QUESTAR PUBLISHERS, INC.

THE LIGHT BEHIND THE STAR
© 1989 by David R. Johnson
Published by Questar Publishers, Inc.

Printed in the United States of America

ISBN 0-945564-14-7

the Light behind the Star

DAVID R. JOHNSON

QUESTAR PUBLISHERS, INC.
Sisters, Oregon

ACKNOWLEDGMENTS

Thomas Womack, for his encouragement,
his editing skills, and his prayers for me.

Don Jacobson, for his prayers and for
taking an unknown policeman and
making him an author.

Jeff Peters of Del Carlo Photo Studios,
for the family photo.

Don Ott, for his help and honesty
in proofing some of my stories.

The men and women who make up
the San Jose Police Department —
and who daily place their lives on the line.

The Family Ministry branch of Campus
Crusade for Christ, for their dedication to
equipping families to face the future.

Dennis Rainey, for taking time out of his busy
schedule to write the foreword to the book.

Carol Fisher, my sister,
for suggesting the book's title.

Kevin Morgan, of the Family Ministry,
for praying for me; his special
friendship warms my very soul.

DEDICATION

to my daughters Michele and Lotte
(who make being a daddy a joy)…

to my wife Maggie
(without her love and encouragement,
this book would not have
been written — I love you!)…

and to my patrol car partner, Jesus Christ…

I dedicate this book and my life.

Foreword

★

THE MEDIA DEPICTS today's law enforcement officers as gun-toting, action-loving, heartless cops who chase down and handcuff murderers and criminals. Although most law enforcement officers do handle their fair share of life-threatening situations, the daily diet of most is saturated with domestic violence. Much of their days are spent solving disputes between spouses or other family conflicts which cannot be worked out without an authority.

It is into this scene that Dave Johnson takes us. *The Light Behind the Star* is no sterile textbook on solving criminal cases and Dave Johnson is no cold-hearted cop. This street cop's heart gripping experiences and glimpses into secret places will move you to place a higher value on your own family relationships.

Dave Johnson is no rookie; with over twenty years of experience on the beat, he tells vividly about places of hurt, despair, violence and destruction. And in a similar style, he gives perspective on how to maintain family unity, and have happiness and purpose in a culture gone wild. Dave not only describes what it is like for a man to live without Christ, but he also tells us how a family can thrive with Him.

★───

If you are like me, your only regret will be that *The Light Behind the Star* is over too soon!

Dennis Rainey
National Director
Family Ministry

Introduction

★

THE QUESTION I'm probably asked most by other Christians is, "How can you be a policeman and a Christian at the same time?" I usually reply, "I don't understand how anyone can be a police officer and *not* be a Christian." Sometimes I continue by telling them about Romans 13:4 — "The policeman is sent by God to help you" (in the *Living Bible* paraphrase).

I guess I take this question as a personal challenge, not only to my Christian walk, but to my chosen profession as well. Most people are influenced by Hollywood's images of a police officer — either a bumbling Keystone Cop, or a cold, heartless, "Dirty Harry." He fights the bad guys, argues with his captain or supervisor, has a nonexistent family life, and pursues an affair with the female co-star. My daily life is much different, and so is that of most police officers. We're just like everyone else. And like other professions, each police department has good cops, not-so-good cops, and cops who can cause others grief.

I am also asked occasionally why I wanted to become a policeman. Maybe part of the answer is my wanting to help people or to make the streets safe for my children. But those replies don't really answer the question enough for me. I just know that God has put me in this unique position, one that requires me to rely on Him every moment in every day.

★————————————————————————————

My job gives me constant contact with people under difficult conditions; in every personal encounter, I hope each person will see not just the light reflecting off the star I wear on my chest, but also the Light coming from behind the star.

I hope these vignettes will prompt you to think about what's important to you, to your family — and to God. If that happens, this cop on the streets of San Jose will be an even happier man.

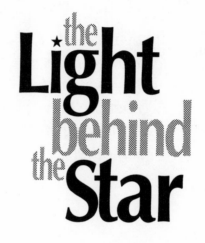

*My eyes couldn't
leave their faces
as they watched
two people they
loved tearing at
each other...*

Death of a Family

★

MY POLICE RADIO INTERRUPTED my usual patrolling with a call for "51-66." I reached for my mike and replied, "Go ahead to 51-66." The operator began dispatching me on a far too familiar call: "Respond on a 4-15 family" (the code for a disturbance). I acknowledged the call and the address, and began heading for the location as the dispatcher assigned another police unit to "fill" (assist) me.

As I gave a "10-9-7" message (arrival at the scene) on the radio, I could see a couple standing in the front yard of the home. The woman was crying and yelling at the man, who was standing with his hands in the pockets of his greasy overalls. I could see homemade tattoos on his arm — usually a sign of having been in prison. I was glad my "fill unit" had arrived as I stepped from my patrol car.

Walking toward the two, I heard the woman demanding that he fix whatever he had done to the car so she could leave. He responded only with a contemptuous laugh.

She turned to me and asked if I would make him fix the car. The other officer came forward, and we separated the couple to find a solution to the problem.

I began talking to the man, who told me his wife was having an affair and was leaving him. I asked if they had gone for counseling, and he said he wasn't interested. He said he was interested only in getting back his "things," which he said she had hidden from him.

I asked the wife about his things, and she said she wouldn't give them to him until she got one of the VCR's. She said she wanted only one of the three VCR's they owned.

The other officer walked over to the wife's car and looked under the hood to see if he could fix the trouble. The husband walked over, took the coil wire out of his pocket, and handed it to the officer. He then told his wife she could have the VCR if he could have his things. She finally agreed and went into the house. (I found out later that his "things" were narcotics he was dealing in.)

As the wife entered the house, I noticed two girls standing in the doorway, watching the drama unfold. They were about eight and ten years old. Both wore dresses, and each clung to a Cabbage Patch doll. At their feet were two small suitcases. My eyes couldn't leave their faces as they watched two people they loved tearing at each other.

The woman emerged with the VCR in her arms and went to the car, where she put it on the crowded back seat. She turned and told her husband where he could find his things. They agreed to divide their other possessions equally.

Then, as I watched in unbelief, the husband pointed to the two little girls and said, "Well, which one do you want?" With no apparent emotion, the mother chose the older one. The girls looked at each other, then the older daughter walked out and climbed into the car. The smaller girl, still clutching her Cabbage Patch doll in one hand and her suitcase in the other, watched in bewilderment as her sister and mother drove off. I saw tears streaming down her face. The only "comfort" she received was an order from her father to go into the house, as he turned to go talk with some friends.

There I stood...the unwilling witness to the death of a family.

As I write this, I sit in my living room with my wife on the couch across from me, while my two daughters, ages eight and ten, lie asleep in bed. We are listening to Cynthia Clawson singing "Softly and Tenderly Jesus Is Calling."

And I cry in my soul for a family that is no more.

I could feel the warmth of her tears on my cheek as they mixed with mine…

So Much for My Saturday

★

I HAD IT ALL PLANNED. There were all those little things around the house that needed to be done — Saturday would be the day! I'd kept it clear on the calendar for weeks.

On the Tuesday before my Saturday, my ten-year-old daughter, Lotte, came to me with tears ready to spill over the edge of her eyes. Her pet rabbit, Leo, wasn't doing very well. We had known for some time that he was having trouble with his hind legs, but now he was beginning to suffer. Lotte had decided it was time to end his pain.

"Daddy, will you take Leo and me to the vet on Saturday?"

Knowing how important it was for her to have someone there with her, I was touched that she wanted me to go instead of her mom. As a matter of fact, I listened as she told Maggie she wanted it to be a "special time" for just her and me.

Saturday finally arrived, and Lotte, Leo and I all got into the car to go to the vet — not what I would call a joyous occasion. It was still early, and I figured I would have at least a good half day to get done all the things I wanted to do.

We arrived at the vet's office around 9:00 A.M., and carried in our rabbit. We waited with him quietly for the doctor.

It was becoming harder than I had expected.

Finally we were called into the examining room. The doctor agreed with our concerns. Leo was suffering, and it would be best to end it.

The lethal medication was given, and Lotte and I held on to each other as it began to flow through Leo. He sat on the examining table as we stroked his soft body and talked to him. We cried as we told him how we were going to miss his running across our backyard to greet us when we came outside, and how we would miss his untying our shoes with his teeth.

Lotte bent down and softly kissed her bunny goodbye. Leo slipped quickly away, and I thought my heart would break as I held Lotte close to me.

We lifted Leo into the box we had brought, and carried him back to our car.

It was 10:30. As I drove home, Lotte held my hand. We weren't talking much, but the communication was there. I suggested we go out for breakfast, one of Lotte's favorite things to do. She said she would like that.

We ate and talked, just the two of us, spending precious moments together — time worth more than a king's ransom, time whose worth couldn't even be calculated in dollars and cents.

We finished breakfast and drove home. It was noon.

I dug a grave for Leo in our backyard, right next to Michele's rabbit which had died several years earlier. We had a little grave-side service with Maggie, Michele, Michele's girlfriend Katy, Lotte, and me. Katy read a little poem she wrote for Lotte and Leo.

It was all too much for Lotte, and she went to

her room and cried. I entered her room and again held her as she released flood gates of grief. We talked more, and just sat quietly with each other.

It was 1:30 P.M. when I finally finished covering Leo's grave.

As I was getting ready to change into my work clothes to mow the lawn, Lotte came into my bedroom. She wanted to know if I would take her to the doll show at the fairgrounds. I thought about the lawn...the car...my workshop — all crying for my attention.

We arrived at the fairgrounds about 2:00, and began walking around looking at the exhibits. Lotte found a collection of stuffed bunnies and fell in love with one dressed in a white and lavender wedding dress. We bought it, and after looking around some more, returned home.

It was 4:15 when I finally changed into my work clothes and went out to begin changing the spark plugs on my car. Michele and her friend Katy came running out and pleaded with me to let them get up into the attic. They wanted to look for some old dolls that were stored there. I finished the spark plugs, and then helped the girls into the attic. We began looking through storage boxes, and found Maggie's high school scrapbooks. We laughed at the hairstyles and clothing. We went through boxes of baby clothes and toys and various things a family accumulates over the years. Then Maggie called up to us: Dinner was ready.

At 6:30 we all sat down to eat. At 7:15, Maggie and I let the girls clean up the dishes while we went for our nightly walk. The air was crisp, and the warmth of Maggie's hand refreshed my heart as we walked our three miles.

A little after 8:00, we arrived home. By the time I laid a fire in the fireplace and picked up my writing paper, it was past 8:30. Michele went with Maggie in the car to take Katy home. Lotte and I were in the living room, where the fire glowed warmly, listening to a tape of praise songs by the Maranatha Singers. I glanced up from my writing and looked at Lotte sitting on the couch. She was dressing her new bunny. Tears were creeping down her cheeks.

I called her name. She looked up, and moved from the couch to my lap. I could feel the warmth of her tears on my cheek as they mixed with mine, and we once again held each other.

I searched for words to comfort my little girl, but instead it was she who spoke the words, words that came from knowing the unconditional love of a father and the perfect love of the Lord. "Daddy," she began simply, "I love you so much. Thank you for going with me today." After a slight pause she added, "It's okay to cry, Daddy. Jesus is so good. He'll take care of us." She was so right.

It's ten o'clock on Saturday night. My list of things to do today is still there. The grass is longer, and the trees still need trimming. My workshop is still a mess. But I look at my two precious daughters as they sleep now in their beds, and I know that I made right choices today. The things on my list are but mere shadows in the light of the needs of my daughters. Praise to the name of Jesus for opening my eyes to see the light — and to not worry about the shadows.

I can still recall that sight of air and motorcycle below. Then everything went blank...

Just Another Morning

★

IT WAS JUST LIKE ANY OTHER MORNING. I got up and dressed for work. I was assigned police motorcycle duty at the time, and the warm July day was a perfect one for riding.

Before leaving home I had my regular time with Maggie and the girls, and then walked to the garage where the motorcycle was parked. I started it, and drove to the front of the house where Maggie stood waiting, as she always did. We said our goodbyes. I leaned over and kissed her, and reminded her that this was my last work day before my vacation was to begin. The two of us were planning to drive up the California coast to Mendocino to celebrate our wedding anniversary.

The warm breeze felt invigorating as I drove the ten minutes to the police station for our pre-shift briefing session. There was nothing unusual about it. I made arrangements to meet another officer for our lunch break, then drove out to my assigned patrol area.

It was just another morning.

I maneuvered my motorcycle through the city traffic. Suddenly a moped shot out from a side street into the intersection without stopping for the stop sign. I cringed as I watched a car swerve and skid to avoid hitting the moped. I could see terror on the

face of the moped driver, who appeared to be only
twelve or thirteen — too young to be operating a
motor vehicle. I made my turn as he continued
racing down the street. I activated my red lights, and
accelerated toward him.

He looked back over his shoulder as he turned
onto another street, running another stop sign and
driving on the wrong side of the road. I couldn't believe it: He was actually trying to outrun me. His motorbike had a top speed of 32 m.p.h., while I could
go from zero to 65 in four and a half seconds, and
had a top speed of 130 m.p.h. I accelerated and was
in front of him in a matter of seconds.

I pointed to the curb and said simply, "Pull it
over."

We were in front of a fenced school yard. He
began slowing down, and angled toward the curb. He
looked at me, then at the school yard, then back at
me. I could read his face. Just as I said, "Don't even
think about it," he accelerated and jumped the curb
and entered the school yard through an opening in
the fence.

I was right behind him.

I feared for his safety as the back wheel of his
motorbike began to slide dangerously back and forth
in the soft dirt. I turned off my siren and let off the
gas, hoping it might be enough to get him to slow to
a safer speed.

We rounded a baseball diamond and entered a
portion of ground with weeds two feet high. He was
headed straight for an opening in the fence which
would take him back to the street. Right in the
middle of the narrow opening was a four-inch pipe
sticking straight up from the ground, and about four
feet high. It was there to prevent people from riding

motorcycles through the opening and onto the school grounds.

The rider slid to a stop and jumped off the bike. He was so frightened he literally picked up the bike and lifted it over the pipe.

I stopped my motorcycle, jumped off, and ran toward the boy as he started the bike, jumped back on, and accelerated. I missed grabbing him by inches.

I knew I couldn't catch him on foot so I ran back to my motorcycle and headed quickly back through the weeds, searching for an alternative exit from the school yard.

I never saw the drainage ditch which my front wheel went in to, but suddenly I found myself airborne — I can still recall clearly that sight of air and motorcycle below me. Then everything went blank.

When I regained my senses, there was a cloud of dirt in the air. I pulled myself up to my knees and tried to breathe, but couldn't. My chest ached. At that moment I truly believed I was about to die.

Slowly I began catching small gasps of breath. I looked at my motorcycle lying about six feet away. The windscreen was destroyed, the radio box and saddlebags shattered, the antenna broken. Nearby were my coat and my papers, which were starting to blow around in the breeze. It all seemed like a bad dream that I wanted to end.

Suddenly a man (an off-duty fireman, I found out later) was standing above me. He suggested I lie back down, and placed my coat under my head. The pain in my chest began to throb.

He ran to my motorcycle and and grabbed the mike. I heard the radio operator answer his call for

an ambulance and a resuscitator. I was amazed that
the radio still worked.

The operator asked who the injured officer was. I
gasped out my call signs to the man. After he relayed
them, the radio came alive with police units re-
sponding.

Within moments I heard sirens. The fire department arrived first and began giving me oxygen.
Police units and the ambulance arrived soon after.
As the medical personnel loaded me into the ambulance I gave a description of the moped rider to several officers, and they left on a search for him. (The
thirteen-year-old boy was apprehended a short time
later at his home.)

On the ride to the hospital, my mind began to
slow down and piece the events together. As I lay
there in agonizing pain, I thought of my Lord, and
prayed: *Lord, You have my undivided attention. What
do You want?* I heard the simple, inward answer immediately: "I want your attention."

As paramedics carried me into the emergency
room, I saw a fellow officer and Christian brother,
Brent Pascoe. He was silent, but concern for me was
etched in his face. (In a letter several days later — a
letter I still treasure — he would put into words his
feelings of concern and his appreciation for the special Christian friendship we had developed over the
years.)

In a short while I was admitted into the hospital's intensive care unit. I had broken all the ribs on
my right side, some in two places. My right lung was
punctured, requiring the insertion of a chest tube
through my broken ribs. I had also broken my right
collar bone.

The next few days are a blur in my memory, as I

was sedated most of the time. But even in the twilight of consciousness I was aware of God's love and presence.

I awoke one night to see nurses and doctors crowding around a bed near mine, treating a woman injured in an accident. As a nurse passed by, I said to her, "She's in real bad shape, isn't she?"

She nodded, then asked if I needed some pain medication. I said yes, but that before taking it I wanted to pray for the woman.

"You want to pray for her?" She looked surprised — and I was a little surprised myself at having spoken the words. As she gave me the injection, I prayed for the woman, slipping into a dark sleep before the prayer was ended.

I awoke the next morning and saw the empty bed against the wall. I didn't have to ask what had happened.

The nurse I had spoken with came to my bed before going off duty, and confirmed that the woman had died soon after I'd gone back to sleep. She also said she was touched that I would pray for a stranger while in so much pain myself. During moments when I was awake the next few nights, I told her of my Savior and Healer.

After being transferred to a recovery floor, I became acquainted with a kind, middle-aged nurse who told me her daughter had been involved years earlier in an automobile accident that left her confined to a wheelchair. She said she was angry with God for what had happened to her daughter, and so did not attend church anymore. We talked often during the week I was in her care.

One day a technician with a blood tray walked in — which didn't surprise me, since I had blood samples drawn several times a day — but she looked a little nervous as she set the tray down next to my bed. She answered my greeting by saying, "I'm not here to take blood." She introduced herself as Sue, and said she had heard at church — the same church I attended — about my accident. "I was just wondering if it would be all right to come in during my breaks to talk with you." None of the people she worked with were Christians, she said, and she just wanted to talk to someone about spiritual things. From then on she came by as often as her schedule allowed, and we talked of our wonderful Savior. It was the beginning of a friendship that has endured through the years, and she is now like one of the family.

Another morning the phone near my bed rang, and Maggie answered it. After a few moments she put her hand over the receiver and said, "It's the mother of the boy who ran from you. She wants to know if she can bring her son here to see you." I said yes, and Maggie relayed the message.

Soon both parents arrived with the boy. He told me he was sorry for what had happened. Then his parents explained that he had taken the motorbike out without their knowledge. Knowing he would get in trouble with them if he got caught, when he saw me he panicked, to say the least. His parents said they had gotten rid of the bike and wanted to know what they could do for me.

Again I felt God's love begin to flow through me. I thanked them for their concern, then spoke directly to the boy. I told him I wasn't angry at him, and held no bitterness for having been injured. I told him I was glad he had not been hit by the car.

"The reason I'm not angry," I said, "is Jesus." I went on to convey His love to these three strangers.

Finally the day came for my release from the hospital. It was a Monday. The nurse whose daughter was in a wheelchair came into my room with her face aglow. She announced that she and her daughter had gone to church the day before, and wanted to begin attending faithfully.

The drive home was exhilarating. Tears of joy came to my eyes as I felt the warm wind in my face, and reflected on how good the Lord had been to me.

Entering the driveway, I saw Maggie's sister at the door with her face beaming, and then the girls ran out to welcome me back. As we walked into the house, I noticed the smell of fresh paint. Bursting with excitement, my sister-in-law told how thirty friends from our church had descended on our house to do some sprucing up and to finish some redecorating we had started — knowing it would be some time before I would be up for doing it myself.

We walked down the hall to our bedroom, where I would be spending much of my convalescing time. We opened the door and could hardly believe our eyes. It was a room fit for a king, with new carpeting (donated by a local carpet store), new wallpaper and matching drapes, and new bed coverings and pillows. Seeing the work of love that had taken place, Maggie and I held each other and cried. Our friends had also redecorated the children's rooms, as well as taking care of the lawn and other routine chores around the house. (Maggie and the girls had been staying at her parents' home, which was closer to the hospital.)

It's now been several years since the accident. At the time it seemed to be the worst experience of my life, but now I can remember it as one of the best times, a blessing in disguise. I still suffer from back problems and a few other effects from the injuries, but as I look back, I can see God's hand in it all. He wanted my attention — and got it.

I came to realize that my plans are not necessarily His plans, and that I need to always be listening for His call. God worked through me during those days to touch lives for His glory and His kingdom, but most of all He used that time to draw me closer to His heart.

And it all began just like any other morning.

They were savoring that moment of life together…

Be Still and Know

★

AS USUAL, TRAFFIC WAS HEAVY on the drive home from work. I began watching with great interest, and a little amusement, as an impatient driver in front of me maneuvered his car from lane to lane in a vain attempt to get ahead. The problem was that as he got into one lane, traffic in it would stop while it started forward again in the other lane. When he switched back, the same thing would happen.

I laughed to myself at the next traffic signal — because stopped right next to me was the same driver, waiting impatiently for the light to change. He picked up a cassette tape from the seat beside him, shoved it into the player, listened for a few seconds, ejected it, threw it down, and grabbed another tape and shoved it into the player. In the thirty-odd seconds it took for our traffic signal to cycle back to green, he changed tapes three times. When the light finally changed, he roared off, changing lanes again in his great quest to catch time.

As I began driving forward, I noticed on the sidewalk a man about thirty years old pushing an empty baby stroller — empty, because walking at his side was a girl of about three or four. She was balancing on the curb with all the precision and concentration of a circus high-wire performer, her steps slow and deliberate. I could see from a quick glance at her daddy's face that he was enjoying every moment.

Without hurry they were savoring that moment of life together, seemingly unaware of the world rushing by them.

They could be unconcerned about catching time because they already had caught it — and were enjoying it as God intends it to be enjoyed.

"Be still," God says, "and know that I am God" (Psalm 46:10).

*...meant just
for me...*

Notes from the Heart

★

I'M NOT SURE WHEN IT STARTED, but ever since it did I've looked forward to my lunch break at work.

It's not that I make great lunches; it's that for some time now, my thirteen-year-old daughter, Michele, has been putting little notes in my lunch box. They're not very long — just special little notes that say things like... "Thank you for taking time to talk with me," "I love you, Daddy, with all my heart," "Jesus loves you and so do I," "I'm praying for you," "Hurry home, I miss you," "Today's assignment: Find something that reminds you of God and tell me about it," "Pray for me in my walk with the Lord," "I love it when you do special things with me," "Everything is in His hands," "I'm proud of my Daddy," "You are a great encouragement to me," "He causes the storm to be still —Psa. 107:29" "Jesus is with you always — He will catch you when you stumble," or "The best part of my day is when you come home." Special notes meant just for me, from the heart of a special daughter.

I'm not sure when it started, but ever since it did I've looked forward to breakfast at home.

It's not that I make great breakfasts; it's that for some time now, my heavenly Father has been giving me little notes to read, notes that warm my very soul, words that give encouragement. Words like, "I am with you always," "I love you," "When you fall, I'll be there to pick you up," and "I have promised you a home in My kingdom." Notes from the very heart of God, meant just for me.

God has notes for you too — notes that say "I love you," and "I'm waiting for you." The only thing you need to do is pick them up and read them, in the morning or the afternoon or the evening (God doesn't care when). He wants you to know they are words from His very heart, meant just for you.

I've left my fingerprints on thousands of places…

Fingerprints

★

DUSTING FOR FINGERPRINTS at the scene of a crime can be a real challenge. Since we don't know where to look for a print, we have to guess the places a suspect would most likely touch.

Then we have to make the prints visible so we can "lift" them. This process is done by taking a very fine brush, dipping it into a fine powder, and then brushing the area we suspect has been touched by the criminal. The powder sticks to the traces of skin oil left behind from a touch of the hand.

The pattern made by the powder on the oil is then picked up with a special tape, and the tape is placed on paper and sent for analysis to our fingerprint department. Computers there can tell us in a matter of seconds who the print belongs to — that is, provided the person's fingerprints are on file.

Occasionally I have lifted some beautiful prints, only to find out they belonged to the victim, or, more embarrassingly, to me.

When I stop to think about it, I've left my fingerprints in thousands of places. I've left them on doorknobs, chairs, tables, and windows. Countless walls were smeared by my hands when I was little, and the smears would still be there if those walls hadn't been painted or washed.

We all touch many things as we travel through

life; we also touch many lives. With each touch —
through a word or deed, as well as through an
actual, physical touch — we leave our mark.

In Matthew 8:3 we read, "And Jesus stretched
out His hand, and *touched* him." We have an obliga-
tion to follow Jesus' example. I believe life as a
Christian means leaving visible fingerprints of an invisible Savior on the lives and souls of mankind, the
same way Jesus left His fingerprints on us. We can
do it through kind words and actions — perhaps
through supporting a missionary, or helping in the
church nursery, or visiting an elderly couple in a
rest home.

My daughters leave their fingerprints of kindness
on, of all places, the neighbors' garbage cans. Every
week they take in the garbage cans from the curb
after the sanitation trucks have come by and emp-
tied them. Hopefully the neighbors will see, along
with my daughters' fingerprints, the fingerprints of
God.

When you stop to think about it...two thousand
years ago God reached down from heaven and
touched the earth — and the print He left is Jesus.

*I wondered
what God could
do with a loser
and sinner
like me...*

His Mighty Hand

★

I COULD NEVER quite get my life together in my pre-teen and teenage years. I struggled with low grades in school and a poor self-image. Try as I would, I could never be number one or even number two in anything I attempted. I was constantly defeated, and at times I was so discouraged I wanted to give up on life completely.

When I was in the fourth grade I had accepted Jesus as my personal Savior one Sunday when I went forward in a church service. I had attended classes at the church for several weeks, so I had a head knowledge of the truth I professed that Sunday morning. I have no doubt my profession was real, and God put His seal on me that morning — but my life didn't reflect the presence of the One who had saved me.

Somehow I made it through high school, but because of low grades I didn't qualify to attend a state university. I enrolled in a local junior college with high hopes of starting from scratch and beginning a new life. I was unaware that God even then was leading me — or should I say, *pushing* me — in the direction of learning complete reliance on Him.

During one class session of my Music Appreciation course, two girls came in and sat near me in a row of seats which gave a good view of the rest of the auditorium. (They later told me they chose that row because they wanted to pick out the best-looking guy in class. I don't remember if the lighting was bad, or if I was the only male there — but, anyway, they picked me.)

Several days later, when the teacher asked us to form discussion groups for working together, these two girls decided I would round out their group. They moved over closer and introduced themselves.

Over the next month, Pam Gerhart and Maggie Cox became my good friends. We went together to lunch and to concerts, and took breaks together between classes.

In time I became aware of a small fire growing in my heart for Maggie. One weekend Pam went out of town for a wedding, and I asked Maggie to go to a show with me. To my surprise, she accepted. After the show we drove to her home and I met her parents and sister. We had a great time laughing and enjoying each other's company. We found out that night that we were both Christians — and we talked about that too.

Pam returned and, for a while, the three of us continued going places together. But soon the three of us became two...and two years later, the two became one.

During our courtship, I attended Maggie's church. God used the young Bible preacher there to speak to me week after week. He spoke of how God had a plan for my life, and I needed to yield my life to Him. I wondered what God could do with a loser and sinner like me. I wondered if God could really forget my past failures. Would He really cast my sins into the sea called "Never to Be Remembered"?

Each time I asked, the answer kept coming back the same: *Yes, I will forgive and forget the past.*

*Trust Me, yield to My will, take My hand and I will
make you into a new vessel for My glory.*

I wish I could say I immediately yielded my whole
heart to Christ, but it didn't happen that way.
Slowly, over the years, I began to give back my life
piece by piece to the One who had given it to me in
the first place. My language, my thoughts, my eyes,
my money, my personal possessions, my marriage —
and yes, finally, all my past sins and failures were
handed over to Christ.

I handed them all over to the One who tells us:
"Humble yourself therefore under the mighty hand of
God, that He may exalt you at the proper time, casting all your anxiety upon Him, because He cares for
you" (1 Peter 5:6-7).

I still make wrong choices and miss out at times
on God's plan, but even in those difficult moments I
know God is there and will not let go of my hand. If I
fall, He's there to put me back on my feet and —
when necessary — to carry me.

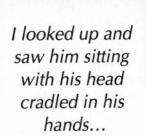

I looked up and saw him sitting with his head cradled in his hands…

The Meeting

★

RAIN WAS JUST beginning to fall, and the streets were getting slick. I decided to head back to the station and exchange my police motorcycle for a patrol car for the rest of my shift. The forecast was for heavy showers, and motorcycles on wet pavement can mean disaster.

I was waiting in one of two left-turn lanes, wishing the red light would change so I could get back to the station and out of the downpour. I was thankful for a large bread delivery truck in the turn lane next to me because it provided a little protection from the wind and rain.

Finally the signal changed. I began easing left and was surprised when the bread truck didn't turn, but instead went straight.

A horn sounded as the truck nearly sideswiped a car in the through lane. I looked to my right, and turned on my rear yellow flashers. I swung the motorcycle right, and slowed — the other traffic also slowed, allowing me to cut across the lanes and follow the truck, which continued accelerating.

As I began gaining on the truck, I watched the next signal light ahead of us change from green to yellow to red. The truck began to slow, but instead of stopping, the driver made a left turn against the red light. Traffic again slowed to avoid a collision. I activated my red lights and began slowly accelerating so I wouldn't lose traction on the now very wet pavement.

My speedometer needle climbed above 45 — we were in a 25-mph zone — and the truck was still pulling away from me.

Up ahead was another red signal, and I wondered if the truck would stop or run that one too. I wasn't sure if the driver just wasn't paying attention, or was trying to outrun me, hoping I'd stop pursuing because of the rain — or maybe hoping I would "dump" my motorcycle.

The truck's brake lights finally lit up and the vehicle stopped at the intersection. I pulled along the driver's side and knocked on the window.

I could tell by the look on the driver's face that he hadn't seen me until that moment. I motioned for him to pull over to the curb on the other side of the intersection. As he did, I pulled behind him.

The driver's side of the truck had a window but no door, so I walked to the passenger's side, where the driver opened the large sliding door. He moved back and asked me in so I could get out of the rain. I stepped inside as he handed me his license.

"I don't know what I did," he said, "but I'm sure you wouldn't have stopped me if I hadn't done something wrong."

As I started writing the ticket, I gave him an account of the violations he had committed and the accidents he nearly caused. I didn't even mention the danger he had put me in, having to pursue him on wet pavement.

I was surprised that he made no response. When I finished talking, I looked up from my ticket writing and saw him sitting with his head cradled in his hands.

"This just hasn't been my day," he said. Then he looked at me. "Officer, I'm not trying to talk my way out of the ticket," he said. "I know I deserve it. But I need to tell someone about what's happened to me today. Would you listen?"

I said I would, and he suggested I finish the ticket first, because what he had to say would take some time. I completed the ticket and gave him his copy.

"Okay," I said. "I'm ready to listen."

He paused for a moment, took a deep breath, and said, "I found out today my mother has cancer. We've known my dad has had it for several months now, but we had no idea about Mom. The doctors have given them both only a short time to live."

I didn't know what to say. The only words that came to mind were ones that often sound phony, but I really meant them: "I'm sorry. I can't imagine how hard that is for you."

The cab of the truck fell silent except for the sound of splashing water from cars passing by, their drivers unaware of the exchange inside between a policeman and a bread truck driver.

Tears were rolling down his cheeks. "That's not all," he said, barely able now to speak. "I just received a call from an attorney. I had no idea what it was about and why he was asking questions, but when I pressed him, he told me my wife had filed for divorce. We've been having problems, but I never dreamed they were that bad.

"What should I do?" he said, turning to me.

I asked if he and his wife had received counsel-

ing. He said they had for a while, but his wife re-
fused to go any more.

"I need help," he said. "Isn't there anything you
can suggest for me?"

Almost before realizing it, I responded, "Yes, I
have a Friend who can help you." I asked if he really
wanted to hear what I had to say, and without hesitation he answered yes. I quickly said a silent prayer
for the right words, then for fifteen minutes spoke of
the love Christ had for him.

He soaked in each word, like the desert drinking
up the rain. When I finished, he said he had never
heard before the idea that Jesus had died just for
him. I asked him if he would like to accept Jesus
into his life right then. He thought for a few moments, then said he wanted to think about it first. I
invited him to come to church with me the next
Sunday and learn more about what I had told him,
and he agreed. We made arrangements to meet in
front of the church.

Before leaving, I asked him if it would be okay if I
prayed for him. Again he said yes, so I did.

As I stepped back into the rain and started
toward my motorcycle, he jumped from the truck
and caught up with me.

"I don't even know your name," he said. I told
him, then he extended his hand and said, "I'm Ron."
Still gripping my hand he added, "Thank you for
taking time to talk to me."

He walked back to his truck, then stopped and
turned and, with a slight smile, called out, "Thanks
for the ticket too!"

On Sunday I stood in front of the church, half expecting Ron not to show. A few minutes before the service was to start, I saw him drive up and park. To my surprise, doors on both sides of the car opened; Ron had brought a friend. He introduced us and I introduced them both to my family, then we all went inside.

During the service I frequently wondered what Ron and his friend were thinking. Did the minister's words make sense to them? As the sermon came to an end, the minister stepped from the pulpit and invited those who had never accepted Jesus as their personal Savior to come forward while we sang a hymn. Before we had sung one line, Ron was out of the pew heading for the front of the church. During the next verse, Ron's friend went forward. Both knelt down and asked Jesus to take control of their lives.

Ron got involved in a Bible study group and began growing in the Lord. His parents died a few months later, and his wife went ahead with the divorce. Through the struggles Ron kept his eyes on Jesus, looking to Him for his strength.

He began attending another church in the area and I eventually lost contact with him. One afternoon while I was on duty, I was stopped in my patrol car at an intersection, and heard someone yell my name. It was Ron, standing on the corner waving to me. Beside him, holding his hand, was a woman. I pulled over and got out, and after Ron and I exchanged greetings he introduced me to his new wife. They had met in a Bible study group and now had been married for more than a year. Ron told me of their church involvement, and how the Lord had been working in their lives.

When it was time for me to go, Ron said, "You

know, the first time I met you, you prayed for me in my bread truck. Would it be okay if I prayed for you right now?" Next to my police car the three of us held hands while Ron prayed to the One who, on a rainy day years earlier, had arranged our first meeting...an encounter in which God had used me as a spark in Ron's life, so He could fan into flame a light that would shine for eternity.

*How could
I know what
God wanted
me to do?*

God's Call

★

I WAS SITTING in a classroom listening to a young woman give her testimony at a conference I was attending. She spoke from notes held in her shaking hand. Her speech wasn't polished, but as I listened to her words, I could feel in my heart I was in the presence of someone who had heard God's call...and had answered.

She said that as a teenager she knew who Jesus was, but didn't want to accept Him as her Savior. Her reason for resisting? She said she knew that if she accepted Him, He would send her to Africa, and Africa was the last place she wanted to go.

She rebelled against everything she knew was right. She got involved in drugs, alcohol, and finally prostitution.

During those rebellious times, she said she could still hear the Lord's persistent voice. Finally, when her life was all but ruined, she accepted His forgiveness and direction...

As I listened to the woman's words, my thoughts went back to my days in Marine Corps boot camp. I saw the need for Christ in the lives of the young men around me. Many of the recruits had never heard the story of Christ's saving grace. Others had heard the story, but didn't think they

*needed Jesus — because now they were
Marines. I felt the urgency of their need to hear
about Christ's love — I knew the majority of them
would soon be going to Vietnam, and some would
not be coming back.*

*I wondered: If I didn't share the Gospel with
my fellow recruits...who would?*

*And I wondered if God was calling me away
from my life's ambition of being a policeman.
After boot camp, when I joined the reserves, did
God want me to go to seminary instead of study-
ing criminal justice? Did He want me to be a
chaplain so I could minister to men in the military?*

*How could I know what God wanted me to
do?*

Now the woman paused and placed her notes on
a table. She looked out the window as if watching
another world go by. When she continued speaking,
she told how she had recovered from her substance
dependency through the help of the prayers of her
family and friends. She said she went back to high
school and graduated, then went on to graduate
from a Christian college.

*When I returned home from my training and
joined up with my local Marine reserve unit, I realized that the men in the unit were just like those
in my training platoon — so many didn't know
Christ, or had rejected Him. The only difference
was that, for twenty-nine days a month, these
men weren't Marines, but were painters, bankers,
contractors, and other professionals.*

*God began revealing to me that He did want
me to be a minister of His word — but I wouldn't
be standing in a pulpit. I would be behind the
wheel of a patrol car, taking the light of Jesus to
the darkness of the city — carrying God's word
into the very homes and businesses where some
of my reserve buddies lived and worked.*

Choking back tears, the woman recalled how God
had molded her into someone who would carry His
word of forgiveness to a distant, lost world...

*I recalled the Living Bible paraphrase of Romans
13:4 — "The policeman is sent by God to help
you." If God sends policemen, then He must first
call men to be policemen. He had called me as
one of those to fulfill that role, and I knew God
doesn't make mistakes. Being a police officer
meant being right where He wanted me, though
at times I might wish I was doing something else.*

God had called her persistently, the woman said.
And when she finally answered, He said to her,
"What if I asked you to go to Africa?"

"I would go," she answered.

So He did...and she did.

It could have slipped through my busy fingers so easily, and been lost forever…

Catching the Moment

★

WHEN I GO to the scene of a traffic accident, a burglary, or an act of vandalism, I try to keep in mind
that the people involved in these events — people
consumed at the moment by fright, anger, or bewilderment — don't realize that, for me, their crisis is
just one of many such events that I handle each day.

If I fail to consider their heightened emotions,
they wrongly perceive me as being cold or callous. To
avoid this wrong perception, when I arrive at a scene
where I don't have to take some quick or immediate
action, I take a moment and let the people verbalize
their anger, fear, or frustrations — which is often ex-
actly what they want most to do at the time. I *listen*
to what they have to say.

It's a process I've tried to perfect over the years,
both on and off the job. I've discovered people like to
talk to me because they know I value what they have
to say. By stopping and taking the time to listen, I'm
able to catch some precious moments which otherwise would have slipped past me.

Recently, my family and three others went for a
week-long camping trip. One day my sister-in-law
began setting up a crafts table, and I volunteered to
help. I really got into the crafts, as well as watching
all the other activities taking place around us. I
could hardly hear a soft, sweet, little voice behind
me, but I could feel the gentle tug on my trouser leg

— my five-year-old niece Jennifer was standing behind me, clutching a large two-leaf clover in her tiny hand.

Jenny stretched her hand high for me to get a good look at it. I thought she was going to tell me how the third leaf had broken off, but instead she said, "Look, Uncle Dave. It's a green butterfly! I found it under that tree."

I looked carefully at the clover, and said, "It *does* look like a butterfly!"

"I know," Jennifer said, and hurried off to show the others her discovery.

I started to give my attention back to the copper designs — but first I paused to watch Jenny go from person to person with her "butterfly." Most observers simply said "Yes," then turned back to their crafts or games.

Finally Jenny showed her discovery to her mother — and I soaked in the sight of a mother's overflowing love for her daughter. Jenny's mommy watched with great delight as her daughter ran off to catch more butterflies.

I was glad I hadn't missed the opportunity to catch a moment that could have slipped through my busy fingers so easily, and been lost forever.

Sometimes we forget our lives are not made up of not just days, hours, and minutes, but of passing *moments*...moments that can't be held onto, but only touched, before becoming a memory.

That touch can be so many things. It may be a smile. Or a kind word. Or feeling the ocean spray on your face.

Or a small hand tugging on your trousers.

From a room at the end of the hall, light seeped from a partly open door. We walked toward the light, and pushed open the door...

Caring

★

ENVELOPES HAD BEEN CLOGGING the mail slot for several days, and several packages were on the front porch behind a planter. The window drapes were closed. The whole house looked as if the owner had left for vacation and forgotten to stop the mail service.

The postal carrier checked with neighbors to see if they had seen the resident, but they hadn't. The neighbors said, however, that she only came out once a week to get groceries.

Still, the mailman knew this was different; she always took in her mail.

He notified police.

Frank, the officer assigned to the call, was already talking to the neighbors in front of their homes when I arrived. The neighbors said the woman was a retired school teacher with no family or friends. Once she retired, she gradually became a recluse. She was rarely seen by anyone, except on her weekly drive to the store.

We asked about friends she might have, and the neighbors said they never saw anyone go into the woman's house, and never saw her with anyone else.

Frank and I went up to the house and pounded on doors and windows. No one responded. The back door had a window in it, so Frank took his night stick and broke a small hole in the glass. He pushed an old and torn curtain out of the way, reached in, and unlocked the door.

As we pushed the door open into a dark kitchen, Frank and I were overwhelmed by the smell of rotting garbage. The grease-covered counters were piled with old food boxes and wrappers, and bits of food. The floor was so covered with filth I couldn't tell if it was tile or wood.

We called out, then continued through the kitchen into the living room, pushing stacks of boxes and clothing out of the way.

From the living room we entered a dark hallway. There we could hear voices coming from a room at the end of the hall, where light seeped from a partly open door. We walked toward the light, and pushed open the door.

There we found the woman. She had died sometime in the past few days. She had been sitting on the edge of her bed, watching and listening to her only friend — which now spilled its unrealistic life of soap operas onto her lifeless ears and eyes.

Here, as in every other room, we found clutter and filth. The woman's bed was so stacked with blankets, boxes, and clothing that, when she died, she was unable to fall over, and simply leaned over onto one of the piles.

I left the room, and walked out of the house to the front yard where the neighbors had gathered. When I told them what we had found, they shook their heads and said how tragic it was. One next-door neighbor said she didn't know the woman's name, and asked me what it was. Others commented about what they did or didn't know about her.

I kept wondering why none of them had taken the time to care about this lonely woman. As a school teacher she had poured her life into caring for future generations, day after day and year after year. Then one day, she retired and found no one to care for her.

"It is *not* good," God says in Genesis 2:18, "for man to be alone." Yet this woman was truly alone. Yes, it is true that someone who wants a friend should *be* a friend; but that doesn't relieve us of our responsibility to care for others. Nowhere does the Bible say we have to wait for others to make the first move before we become their caring friend. The story of the Good Samaritan in Luke 10 tells us something much different about what it means to be a neighbor.

After I left the woman's house and went back on patrol, I felt a little condemning of her neighbors. Most of them were retired and, in my thinking, had no excuse for not reaching out to her.

When I got home from work that night I told Maggie about the school teacher and her neighbors. We talked about what a tragedy it was for someone to die so completely friendless and alone.

We also talked about our neighborhood...and we were pretty proud of ourselves for at least knowing the names of the people on our street, some of whom had become our good friends. I should have thought about Proverbs 16:18 — "Pride goes before destruction, and a haughty spirit before a fall."

Maggie, meanwhile, had volunteered to be a precinct walker for a local Christian candidate for public office. She requested our own neighborhood since she was familiar with the people. She had been assigned 150 homes. A few days after my encounter with the schoolteacher's neighbors, she set out on the task. After three hours, she returned and dropped, exhausted, onto the couch.

"Do you have any idea how many lonely people there are in our neighborhood?" she asked me. Maggie had only made it around the block, because she kept finding lonely people who wanted someone to talk with, people desperately wanting someone to care for them.

One of our neighbors told Maggie his wife had died several months earlier. We hadn't even known.

I began thinking again of the school teacher's neighbors whom I had been critical of in my thoughts — and I knew I had to include myself with them. Lonely people around me were crying out for a few minutes of caring from someone like me — people desperate for light in a dark world — and I hadn't heard them.

Jesus said in Matthew 5:16, "Let your light so shine before men, that they may see your good works, and glorify your Father who is in heaven." I guess instead of staying inside my house with the light Jesus gave me, it's time I walked around the block with it.

Did he wonder how many people would find such warmth here?

Campfires

★

ONE OF THE things I like best about camping is the evening campfire. When the sun has slipped from the sky and the cool evening blankets the forest, the smell of the fire's smoke, the crackling of the burning wood, and a cup of hot chocolate all make for a special feel.

On a recent camping trip with several families, the weather was cool and we kept a fire going most of the time. The fireplace we used wasn't spectacular to look at — it had been built in the 1920's out of rocks from a nearby creek, held in place by mortar. The years of use had taken their toll — many of the rocks were chipped, and some of the mortar had fallen out.

I noticed that at almost any time, people would be warming up in front of the fire, or just poking a stick in the burning embers. No one had designated the fireplace as our main gathering place — it just happened.

It made a great setting for our morning devotions, as we all sat around the fire, enjoying the fragrance of burning oak and walnut, and listening to messages from God's Word that were meant to kindle a living fire in our souls.

When evening came, we gathered again around the fire to sing songs, perform skits, and roast marshmallows. Each night a family of raccoons stopped by to see our evening show. They would stay for a snack, then scamper off to another camp site to see if someone else's entertainment was better — but they always made it back to our fire in time to catch the closing act.

After the children were in bed, the adults would regather around the fire and stay until the last embers were only a glow. More than once, as Maggie and I reluctantly walked away for the night, I would look back at the faint light which seemed to be beckoning me back for just a few more warming minutes.

Our week went by quickly. We decided to have our last meal around the fire. We wrapped potatoes in foil and nestled them in the hot coals. Then we barbecued steaks.

When it was time to eat, we removed the potatoes from the fire and saw that their foil coverings were all burnt and ash-covered. We all wondered what the potatoes would look like when we opened the foil. The first potato was unwrapped and cut open — perfect! The fireplace had once again delivered a special gift.

After the meal, we packed our gear. I made a final check through the campsite to pick up any missed trash, then stopped at the fireplace to make sure the fire was completely out. I stirred around the ashes. I could feel warmth still radiating from the rocks. The fireplace seemed to call me to stay a minute longer, to build one more fire...sing one more song...tell one more story...roast one more marshmallow...make one more memory.

I wondered about the person who built the fireplace, and what his thoughts were after he laid the last stone. Did he look at it and wonder how many people would find such warmth here? Or did he never give it a thought, as he simply completed the job he was being paid to do, and then left?

Standing there, I realized how important it is to consider the long-term results of what I do each day. Will what I do today bring warmth not only to my children, but to their children, and theirs? Will the fireplace of memories that we build now last for future generations to gather around and enjoy?

As I walked away, I was reminded to build my home like a fireplace to hold warmth for eternity — constructed with the Rock of Jesus, and the mortar of God's word.

*We heard
anxious voices
calling out for
the girl…*

'I'm Not Lost'

★

WE WERE ON a hiking expedition, eight adults and twelve children. It wasn't going quite like we had planned it. Our idea was for everyone to hike in family groups, so we could keep better track of everyone. But some of the older children hiked ahead on a trail that was steeper than the one we intended to follow.

Somehow we managed to arrive at the same point — not at the same time, mind you, but we all made it. There by a river we relaxed; some skipped rocks across the water while others climbed and rappelled on a nearby rocky cliff. While the dads and children were doing the physical things, the moms were sitting on the shore, solving the problems of the world — and of their husbands.

Finally we started back for our campsite to fix the noon meal.

Later, where two trails came together, we stopped to regroup. While there, Maggie asked if I had our camera. I didn't. We checked with our daughters, but they didn't have it either. We figured the only place it could be was back at the river where we had rested.

I wasn't thrilled about having to walk back, but with Maggie along I figured we could have a little time alone as we walked.

75

At the river we found our camera, as expected. As we headed back we were startled to see one of our group's younger members — an eight-year-old girl —walking toward us. We asked where her" buddy" was (we told all the children to always hike in pairs or groups, and never alone). She said her buddy didn't want to come with her, so she decided to go alone.

We told her she was hiking in the wrong direction, but she said she knew where she was going. We tried to explain that she was lost, and that it was a good thing we had run into her. "I'm not lost," she said. Finally we insisted that she come with us.

As we neared the area where we had left the others, we heard anxious voices calling out for the girl. We recognized her mother's voice, and called back to let her know her daughter was safe.

When the girl saw her mother she began crying, while at the same time trying to convince her mother she hadn't been lost. I wondered how she could think that, when it was so obvious to the rest of us. Finally, though, she admitted that she'd been lost — and scared as well.

When I thought about the incident later, I saw it as an illustration of many people today who head off in directions that they think will bring them fame and fortune. When they arrive, they're still unsatisfied, and head down another trail, still looking to find happiness. If someone should mention to them that they're headed in the wrong direction, they get indignant.

Yet God is faithful to warn us: "There is a way which seems right to a man, but its end is the way of death." (Proverbs 14:12).

I'm so grateful that when I was lost, I had a Heavenly Father who didn't let me continue wandering on the wrong path. He persisted in showing me that I would only get more lost and confused if I didn't turn around. In His wisdom He took me by the hand and led me out of the darkness of self, and onto the path of His light.

I wondered if they thought they were about to die...

Growing Pains

★

I ALWAYS LOVE the spring. The hills around the Santa Clara valley where I live change from spots of green and brown to a blanket of lush green velvet that stretches as far as the eye can see. The days get longer, and the buds on the trees begin opening and spraying their sweet fragrance into the soft, warming California breeze.

Early in spring I make my annual trip to the local nursery to pick up several flats of plants to place around our yard. I love the feel of the rich dirt in my fingers as I work the soil. I try not to be involved in anything that remotely resembles police work while I'm off duty, and gardening is right up there as one of my most enjoyable ways of relaxing. Maggie likes the idea too, because she gets to enjoy the blooming flowers outside her kitchen window all summer.

One day while I was planting, I felt a little guilty as I removed the plants from their plastic containers. The plants were three or four inches tall, each bearing at least one flower. Grouped together, the plants looked so beautiful and healthy. But I was separating them from their home and from each other.

As I tried to ease each plant out of its secure environment, its roots clung to the container walls in a final attempt to stay. Some of the roots, which had grown and wrapped themselves into every available cranny, tore off and were left behind. I wondered if the plants thought they were about to die as a result of being uprooted and taken away from the plants with which they'd grown up.

All too often during my annual spring planting, I run out of flower bed space, so three or four plants end up staying in the plastic containers until I can figure out what to do with them. I water them when I water the other plants and feed them plant food when I feed the others. But those in the plastic containers never seem to develop like the ones transplanted in the dirt. Soon the container plants turn brown, lose their leaves, and die, while the garden plants are reaching up to the sun.

I didn't understand why this happened until I looked carefully at the dead plants and found they had become root bound. The plastic containers were fine when the plants were young and needed confinement and protection to get started, but as they grew and developed, their needs changed. In the containers, their roots couldn't lengthen and deepen, so the plants weren't getting necessary nourishment, even though I fed and watered them.

And yet, I suppose, they were happy when I had left them right where they were.

How much like these plants we can be! When our Heavenly Father wants to transplant us, we resist. We don't like being pulled up from our safe environment — our home, church, or job. We're content staying right where we are.

Many of us think we know what's best for ourselves, so we cling to our little containers. The result: Little or no growth.

I wonder: When harvest time comes, which flowers will the Gardener pick first? Which flowers will be displayed in a place of honor, to radiate His handiwork?

Dear Heavenly Father,

You are the Master Gardener of the universe.

You alone know where I'll grow best. Plant me

where You know my roots can grow deep in Your word

and where I can lift up my branches to praise You.

Lord, if You see that I am resisting, tug harder

until I let go of my container, so I can grow

in the security of Your mighty hand.

Amen.

*They had
God's assurance
that someday
they would all
be together
again...*

Cornerstone

★

AS A POLICE OFFICER, through the years I've often been involved with families at the death of a loved one. I've been called to homes where the elderly have died, and where small children have died. I've gone to grieving families when the loved one's death was from natural causes, when it was from an accident, and when it was suicide. No two cases are alike.

I never know how the next of kin will react when I arrive at their home at such a stressful time. I've had doors slammed in my face. And I've been held onto as if I'm a long lost relative.

I've seen that a person's death can either pull a family together, or drive family members apart. They either reach out to each other, or lash out at each other. I've actually seen relatives in the same room as the deceased, arguing over who gets what or who should be in charge.

I've left homes disgusted and angry over what I witnessed inside. I've also left homes knowing that God's strong, tender arms were wrapped tightly around the family, holding it together. These were the families who had God's assurance that someday they would be united again.

Only the right foundation, the right cornerstone, can give a family that kind of peace — "Christ Jesus himself being the cornerstone, in whom the whole building, being fitted together, is growing into a holy temple in the Lord; in whom you also are being built together into a dwelling of God in the Spirit" (Ephesians 2:20-22).

It seems pretty clear! With Christ as the cornerstone, the family will not only survive, but also grow closer to one another and to the Lord Jesus, their Architect and Builder.

With a foundation like that, nothing can topple such a family.

Not even death — for in Jesus, death is already defeated.

'She's going
to be okay,
isn't she?'

'Mom, I've Gone for a Walk'

★

SHE WAS SIXTEEN years old. She was wearing fashionable tennis shoes and jeans. The "in" rock group's picture decorated the T-shirt she was wearing.

I looked around her, at the posters of the latest rock and roll stars on her bedroom walls. Records from the newest singers and groups were stacked neatly on the floor.

I left her bedroom and softly closed the door behind me.

I walked down the hallway to the living room where the girl's mother sat on the couch. I picked up an afghan from another chair and spread it across the woman's trembling shoulders.

Without saying a word, I sat down next to her and looked into her face. Tears sat on the edge of her eyes like water from a dam ready to spill over.

"She's going to be okay, isn't she?" her mother asked.

I searched my mind for the right words to ease the mother's pain, but my mind was like a closed dictionary.

"I'm sorry, but your daughter is gone."

As the tears began to flow down her cheeks, she grabbed my arm and asked in an almost pleading

87

way, "Are you sure? She's only sixteen and it's almost Christmas. She can't be gone! Are you sure?"

I thought, *What could go so drastically wrong for a sixteen-year-old girl to get to the point of taking her life — to become another teenage suicide statistic?*

I asked her mother if the girl had been depressed lately. She paused for a few moments, then said, "No, but she hasn't smiled much lately."

I asked if maybe her daughter had recently had a fight with a friend or boyfriend. She said her daughter didn't have a boyfriend that she knew of, and she didn't have many friends. She said her daughter mentioned that she wasn't popular at school, and that some of the kids made fun of her, and it bothered her.

"Did you talk together about her feelings — about not being popular at school?"

The mother said she didn't think it was very important, so she never mentioned it.

She paused and stared out the window.

"I guess I didn't talk to her very much about anything. She was always gone, or I was at work."

I asked if her daughter had left a note or letter. Her mother handed me a small piece of paper folded in half. I unfolded it and looked at the words scrawled across the page. The note read simply, "Mom, I've gone for a walk." The girl's name was signed below.

Surely there's more, I thought. In most of the suicide cases I've handled, lengthy notes were left explaining feelings of complete hopelessness, of how they felt suicide was the only way to end their suffering and loneliness.

I held the girl's note in my hand and stared at the words. *This can't be all she had to say.*

I thought of the common thread I've seen binding all the cases I've handled involving young suicide victims. It's the thread of communication and acceptance — or, more correctly, the *lack* of communication and acceptance. So many times I've sat with a devastated parent who cries out about how sorry they were to have not taken enough time to be with their child, and how they didn't even realize anything was wrong.

While finishing up the case the next day, I stopped by the school the girl had attended. I spoke with two of her teachers. They said she was a good student, but never seemed to quite fit in with the other kids. Her family wasn't wealthy like most of the other students' families, and her mother was a housekeeper for some of the student's parents. And somehow, this made a sixteen-year-old girl unworthy to be their friend.

As I left the school, I wondered if any of those students knew or cared that she had been crying out for help in their midst for someone to care for her, someone she could call a friend, someone she could tell, "I need to talk with someone — would you go for a walk with me?"

And I thought about all the people, young and old, who are crying out for someone to talk with and walk with — but their pleas fall on deaf ears in a world where, if you aren't one of the beautiful people, you're unworthy of being a friend.

"God sees not as man sees," we read in 1 Samuel 16:7. "For *man looks at the outward appearance*, but the Lord looks at the heart." The "world" dwells on the rich and the outwardly beautiful. That puts the responsibility on us Christians of reaching out to the lonely and hurting people around us.

They may only say, "I've gone for a walk."

But you can be sure there's more.

The dispatcher alerted us: "The lost boy has been located — in the next-door neighbor's swimming pool.'

Getting Involved

★

FRANK AND I had just finished a call, and climbed into our police cars. It was nearly time to head to the police station to go off duty.

As I started my car, I heard the police radio call out Frank's unit number. The dispatcher reported a young boy missing from his residence. I heard the address and a description: two years old, wearing tennis shoes, coveralls and a light blue T-shirt. The dispatcher said the mother had lain down on the couch and fallen asleep, and discovered the boy missing when she awoke fifteen minutes later.

Frank acknowledged the call, and began driving to the address. I picked up my radio and told the dispatcher I would respond to the area to help in the search.

Finding lost children can be quite a challenge. In the past I've searched for several hours, only to find out the child's mother had forgotten that Grandpa was going to pick the child up from school and go to the shoe store...or that the child was at a neighbor's house playing and didn't tell his mother because she was asleep and he didn't want to wake her. We also have to consider that the child may have been kidnapped by a stranger, or by a divorced or separated parent.

I was driving directly behind Frank's car. Our

sergeant, Dennis Busch, had also heard the call and, because he was nearby, radioed back that he would also respond.

Suddenly the dispatcher alerted Frank, Dennis, and myself: "The lost boy has been located — in the next-door neighbor's swimming pool."

Adrenaline shot through my veins as I reached for the control switch to activate my red lights. I saw Frank's lights jump on at the same time. We both accelerated. I began praying that the people who found the boy knew CPR — cardio-pulmonary resuscitation — and were attempting to revive him.

As Frank and I rounded the corner near the address, we saw several men and women standing on the sidewalk in front of a house. Dennis was just getting out of his police car and talking with the group of people. As I began getting out of my car, I suddenly saw Dennis bolt toward a gate on the side of the house. As Frank and I got closer, one of the men pointed and told us what he must have told Dennis: "The boy's in the pool in that back yard." I could hardly believe what I'd heard.

Frank and I both ran through a narrow side yard that led to the swimming pool. As we rounded the corner of the house we could see Dennis pulling the boy's limp body out of the pool, lifting him by the back of the shirt.

Dennis laid the boy on the cold cement at the pool's edge and began administering CPR, and Frank knelt down to help.

With Frank and Dennis hovering over the motionless body, attempting to breathe life back into the child, I was left with nothing to do except watch — which is hard for most police officers to do in a life-and-death situation. Unable to help, I searched the boy's face, looking for any sign of life that might flicker there. *If only I could do something...*

Dennis continued to breathe for the boy, while Frank kept compressing his small chest, trying to get his heart going again.

My eyes fell to the coveralls that hung wet on his little body. I thought how much they looked like the ones my girls wore when they were that age. I saw the small tennis shoes on his limp feet, and noticed that one was untied. I wondered if he would ever have someone tie his shoes again.

I tried desperately to choke back the lump tightening in my throat, and could feel tears coming down my cheeks.

I turned, walked a few steps, and took out my handkerchief to wipe my eyes. As I put it back in my pocket, I saw four men standing and watching Dennis and Frank at work. I recognized them as part of the group standing out front when we arrived.

I felt anger welling up inside me. "Who found the boy in the pool?" I asked.

They looked at me, but none of them said a word.

I repeated the question, surprised at how loud my voice came out. Then I continued, "Why did you just leave him in the pool? *Why didn't you at least pull him out?*"

They only hung their heads, and stared at the ground.

Just then the fire department arrived. Soon an oxygen mask was secured around the small face that hadn't changed expression. The firefighters took over the CPR. Dennis was still kneeling, softly stroking the boy's small, closed hand, and staring into his lifeless face.

It's so hard to stand by...

I wondered if it would have made any difference if we had been a little closer, and arrived sooner.

I looked up again at the four men still standing in their group. Suddenly, as if directed by some unseen instructor, they all turned and walked out of the yard, none of them saying a word.

I heard the siren of the approaching ambulance. Soon paramedics surrounded the boy, preparing quickly to take him to the hospital. "I think it's too late," one of them said. "But we'll continue CPR on the way."

The ambulance disappeared from sight, and I turned and looked at the faces of the people left behind. I saw Dennis talking with the boy's mother, who had just arrived and was hurriedly getting ready to go with a friend to the hospital. Several neighbors were close to her, attempting to comfort her with words of encouragement. I think we all knew in our hearts that the boy was gone, but no one wanted to release any last glimmer of hope.

Frank was talking with a group of neighbors to gather any further information for the accident report.

The four men I had seen, meanwhile, were now huddled across the street, apparently trying to avoid getting involved, yet wanting to see and hear what was going on.

I drove home carrying the boy's death inside me, still grieving that a child's life slipped away while people stood by. I didn't think I would ever understand it.

The next morning I picked up my Bible to contin-

ue a study of the book of John. I was in the nine-
teenth chapter, reliving the crucifixion of Jesus
through the words of the apostle John — who had
been there, and was now describing the scene in
such detail.

I could picture in my mind the soldiers dividing
up Jesus' clothing, then casting lots for the seamless
tunic they admired, with no concern for its owner.

I saw men huddled below the cross, mocking
Jesus.

I could see Christ hanging there, suffering, dying.

I could picture Joseph of Arimathea, a man never
mentioned in the gospels until after the crucifixion,
gently taking Jesus down from the cross — along
with Nicodemus, who had once gone by night to talk
with Jesus. I saw these two men struggling with the
limp and lifeless body. I wondered why *they* were
doing this, instead of the twelve disciples. Where
were the disciples? Where was Peter, the Rock, who
said he would die with Jesus? Where were his strong
hands when they were needed? Where was Andrew
or James or Thomas? Why weren't they there? Why
didn't they get involved?

I saw the body of Christ being prepared for
burial, then placed in the tomb. But the disciples
weren't there.

And I realized: Getting involved is a risk. The disciples would have been risking their own lives if they
had gotten too involved at the crucifixion.

Getting involved is risky for us too. When we tell
a neighbor or fellow worker about the love of Christ,
for example, we risk rejection and humiliation. We
have all the excuses we need — we don't have the

time, or the ability — so we don't take the risk. If our conscience starts bothering us about it, then we try the no-risk "involvement" of simply sending our money.

To find a model for getting involved, I need only look to our Savior. I see that to call ourselves followers of Jesus, we have no choice but to get involved in the lives of others. For when God became flesh, He walked among us and with us. He got involved in our everyday cares and needs.

And it was risky. Jesus made that very clear — on a cross.

He said, "This is My commandment, that you love one another, just as I have loved you. Greater love has no one than this, that one lay down his life for his friends..." (John 15:12-13).

*He looked at me
and the others.
'What's wrong?'
he asked...*

Joy Comes in the Morning

★

I WASN'T WORKING my own beat that day. And the first call of the morning was a 10-55 — a deceased person.

The dispatcher informed me over the radio that the fire department was already there and waiting for my arrival.

After driving to the address, I parked my police car behind the fire truck. The fire captain was outside, and said to me, "I don't envy you on this one." He said a nineteen-year-old mentally handicapped boy had died in his sleep.

A fireman greeted me at the door of the home, and introduced me to Mrs. Miller, who was surprised to see me there. I assured her my presence was routine, that police officers were called to all deaths where a doctor wasn't present. She smiled and said she understood, then pointed to a door. "Billy is in, his room." I went to the door, opened it, and stepped inside.

Mrs. Miller had followed me. "He's with Jesus now," she said. We both stood there, saying nothing. My heart told me to pay attention — that I was witnessing something of eternal value. I noticed a Bible on Billy's bed stand, Christian tapes on top of a tape player, and framed Bible verses on the walls. Then we stepped back out, and I closed the door.

The front door opened and two women entered, walked to Mrs. Miller, and hugged her. Mrs. Miller assured them she was fine and that Billy was with Jesus. As the women went to the living room and sat down, Mrs. Miller turned to me and suggested we go into the kitchen. There she asked if I wanted a cup of coffee — "I'm going to make a pot anyway, so it won't be any trouble." I accepted her offer, and watched as she moved about the kitchen as if nothing out of the ordinary had happened. I was surprised at how comfortable I felt sitting at her table.

She told me how Billy had been born with a serious illness, and doctors said he would more than likely die before he reached the age of ten.

We were interrupted as more people arrived at the front door. Mrs. Miller greeted them as she had the first women, and invited them to sit in the living room. She returned to the kitchen, smiled at me and said, "I'd better make a big pot."

She continued talking, explaining that she and her husband decided they would raise Billy as if he were "normal." Billy attended a special school, but otherwise his childhood was like other children's.

She described how outgoing Billy was, and that if others made fun of him, "he smiled at them and said that Jesus loved them, and so did he.

"We knew," she continued, "that the most important thing we wanted to teach Billy was about Jesus. So we did — and Billy loved Him."

One of the women entered the kitchen and asked if she could help, then added that she had overheard the last part of our conversation. She recalled how she had seen Billy talking to strangers and asking them if they knew Jesus. "It was the most important thing in his life," she said, tears welling up in her eyes. Mrs. Miller stepped over and hugged the woman as she cried.

More people arrived and settled in the living room to talk, as I worked at the table on my written report while awaiting the coroner's arrival. I realized that the police form I was completing — "just the facts" — didn't allow me to record the story of Billy's death as it should be written. I wrote, "His room was clean and neat," and, "There were no outward signs of physical trauma to the deceased." But there was no place to mention that his room and the memories he left behind all reflected his love for God, or that I knew he was now at peace in the arms of his Savior.

I got up and walked to the front of the house, still thinking about the report, when my attention was drawn out the window to a man approaching the house. He looked confused as he hurried to the door and opened it. As he stepped inside, he looked at me and the others. "What's wrong?" he asked.

For a moment we were all silent; then Mrs. Miller entered and spoke her husband's name. "What happened?" he asked her.

Choking back tears, Mrs. Miller gently told him about their son. They held onto each other as their tears mingled together. As they stood there, I heard Mr. Miller saying softly, "Thank you Lord. Thank you Jesus." They walked into the kitchen to be alone.

Later they came back into the living room and Mrs. Miller introduced me to her husband. Then the coroner arrived, and when I finished assisting him, I walked back to the living room. Everyone there was now standing in a circle holding hands, recalling how Billy had touched each of their lives. "He loved to sing," one of them said. "We never knew where or when he would just suddenly burst into a song to praise God."

After the coroner left, taking Billy's body with him, I told the Millers goodby. They walked out with me, and we stood together by my patrol car.

"I have a question for you," Mrs. Miller said. "How did they know to send a Christian policeman?"

I smiled and said, "They didn't," and explained that this wasn't even my regular beat; I "just happened to be assigned here."

As I drove away, I pictured in my mind the Millers crying together, not in anguish, but in joy.

And I thought of the words in Psalm 30 — "His favor is for a lifetime. Weeping may last for the night, but a shout of joy comes in the morning."

He was excited to see us and called us by our names. I noticed he was wearing his plastic police badge...

Tommy

★

THE BELL OVER THE SHOP DOOR rang, and I looked up from my dish of frozen chocolate yogurt.

A stooped-over man entered and shuffled across the tile floor, his steps slow and measured. I guessed him to be in his late fifties to mid-sixties.

His baseball cap only partially hid a scalp covered with dry, flaky skin. His face was blotched red, not only from the heat, but also from a skin disorder. His stomach hung over his belt, and his pant legs were dragging the floor as he walked. His shirt tail hung free, and on his shirt pocket was pinned a paper name tag that said "Tommy." In his hand he clutched a metal lunch pail covered with stickers that advertised a local radio station. "Tommy" had all the outward signs of being mentally handicapped.

I wish I could say I spoke with him and asked how he was doing. But like the others in the shop, I tried to ignore the man. I went on eating my yogurt and talking with Frank, the other officer with me. We enjoyed the cool break we were able to get in two or three times a week during the hot summer.

From the corner of my eye I watched as Tommy dug into his pants pocket and laid the change on the counter for the store clerk to count. She asked what flavor of yogurt he wanted, then served him. Tommy sat down at one of the empty tables.

A small child at another table pointed at Tommy and asked, "What's wrong with that man, Mommy?" Others who came in saw Tommy sitting there, and then either bought their yogurt and left, or sat as far away from him as possible.

Frank and I finished eating and talked to a couple of children who wanted to "say hi to the nice policemen." I gave each of them one of the small plastic police badges I carry in my shirt pocket for just such an occasion.

As we started to leave, Tommy got up and walked over. He had yogurt around his smiling mouth. He stuck out his hand and said, "My name is Tommy."

I reached out and took his hand. The roughness of his diseased skin made me want to retrieve my hand as quickly as possible, but Tommy wouldn't let go. He just continued smiling and shaking. He said he liked policemen and wanted to be one.

I told him my name, and introduced him to Frank. Now Tommy released the grip on my hand and grabbed Frank's, and again held on and continued shaking. Finally we were able to get Tommy to release his grip, and we started out the door.

Tommy was right behind us. We turned around to him. Still smiling, he asked, "Can I have a badge too?"

I reached in my shirt pocket and pulled out the last one I had. Tommy's eyes lit up as he pinned it to his pocket. He thanked us, then walked back into the store to finish his yogurt.

Several days later, we made it back to the frozen yogurt shop and, sure enough, Tommy came in. He was excited to see us and called us by our names. I noticed he was wearing his plastic police badge right above his name.

He shuffled to the counter, and dug into his pocket. All he could pull out were some pieces of paper. I got up from the table, stepped to the counter, and asked Tommy what he wanted. "I'll buy it for you," I said.

He thanked me, then sat at his table and enjoyed his yogurt.

Over the next few months, Frank and I took turns buying Tommy his yogurt. We actually began looking forward to our times with him. He would sit at our table and tell us all about his day at the handicapped center where he worked.

Along with the ever present police badge, he occasionally wore a sign pinned to his shirt that told of some special award he had won: "First Place for Can Smashing," or, "First Place for Cleaning My Area." He was proud of his accomplishments, and excited to share them with us.

One day he wore a rather large colored sign that read "Today Is My Birthday." It was his sixty-second birthday — and we celebrated with him.

One hot afternoon the dispatcher radioed a report to Frank of a possible drunk lying by the side of a store. I was close by, so I stopped to assist. When I got out of my car I saw a figure half lying and half sitting on the ground, with people walking quickly past him and pushing their children along to avoid any contact with him. I recognized the lunch pail — and then Tommy. He wasn't drunk, only overcome by the heat. His face was bathed in perspiration and his shirt was soaked through.

"Are you okay?" I asked, coming closer.

Tommy said only, "I fell down."

Frank and I helped him into the patrol car. Frank then drove him to his group home, where he found out Tommy had arthritis in both legs, which from time to time caused them to simply give out, making him fall.

Tommy recovered and was back on his feet in a few days.

The days turned into weeks, and the weeks into months. One day Frank and I realized we hadn't seen Tommy for some time. We decided to stop by his house and see how he was. While on our way there, I received a call for service, so Frank went on to Tommy's by himself.

Afterward Frank told me that he arrived just as a bus pulled to the curb in front of the group home. He watched as the driver helped Tommy out. His arthritis had become worse, and now he could hardly walk without help.

Tommy was overjoyed to see Frank. He kept telling the other residents gathered around that Frank was his friend. Having a policeman for a friend made him an instant celebrity at the home.

We still visit Tommy from time to time, trying to spread a little sunshine in his life. (He especially likes it when we show up with a dish of frozen chocolate yogurt.) We've also found that Tommy puts quite a few rays of light into our lives too.

There are so many "Tommys" in the world today. We see them in our churches, at work, and in our

neighborhoods — people who are mostly alone. I believe they're among the people with whom Jesus was
identifying in Matthew 25 — "I was hungry... I was
thirsty... I was a stranger... I was naked... I was
sick... I was in prison..."

You reach out to them in the same way Jesus
said: "You gave me something to eat... you gave me
drink... you invited me in... you clothed me... you
visited me... you came to me..."

You can touch the lives of others with a simple
act like taking a plate of cookies to the neighbor
down the street, or inviting a fellow worker to lunch.

And if you're really pressed for ideas...take a dish
of chocolate yogurt to Tommy. I know he'd like it —
and you'd really like him.

As I hung up the phone, a wave of disappointment crashed over me, as it had so many times in the past...

Disappointment

★

I HAD RECOMMENDATIONS from past and present supervisors, and they said I should be able to get the new position without much trouble. I had studied the material and memorized the necessary criminal sections. And after the test, I was told it looked like I had it.

Then, while on patrol one afternoon, I was asked by the radio dispatcher to phone the sergeant in charge of the position I had applied for. I drove to the nearest police call box and dialed the number.

My stomach twisted into a giant knot as I heard several rings on the other end. Finally a secretary answered, then put me on hold while she contacted the sergeant. After what seemed an hour, he was on the line.

I told him who I was, and he began his response by telling me how much he wanted me for the position. But he said I had placed second in the testing process, behind an officer with ten years less experience than I. So I wasn't chosen.

As I hung up the phone, a wave of disappointment crashed over me, as it had so many times in the past. It brought back all the disappointing feelings I remembered growing up — the time I wasn't chosen for the Little League baseball team... the time I wasn't chosen to be line leader in the fifth grade...

the time I wasn't chosen captain of the cross country team. And then there were the five other times I hadn't been chosen for police department positions I had applied for over the years. Now, here I was again, not being chosen.

Maggie and the girls greeted me at the front door that afternoon with their smiles and hugs, and told me how glad they were I was home.

"How was work?" Lotte asked.

"Fine," I said.

But I looked at Maggie, and I knew she wasn't fooled.

After the girls left the room, I told Maggie the news, and how I felt about being rejected again.

"You know," Maggie said, "your significance doesn't revolve around your job. You need to look to what you know is really true." (Don't you hate it when someone tells you something like that just when you're ready to have yourself a good pity party?)

I knew Maggie was right, but I still struggled with the disappointment. I knew I needed to deal with it before depression sneaked in and robbed me of my self-worth and joy.

My hands stroked the soft corduroy cover of my Bible. I then tenderly thumbed through the pages, as I also searched the corners of my mind for the Scripture I knew was hidden there just for me.

Finally, there it was — words spoken not by man, but by the living God Himself; words spoken and recorded nearly two thousand years ago, and meant for me today.

My disappointment melted into a puddle and evaporated as I read the words of Jesus to His disciples in John 15:16 — "You did not choose Me, but I chose you and appointed you that you should go and bear fruit and that your fruit should remain."

God chose *me!* — not because I had passed a test or done something worthy, but because He loved me.

Maggie was so right: "Look to what you know is really true."

I realized anew that I was where God had put me, right in the middle of His will, in the place He had chosen.

And right where I wanted to be.

I didn't even realize it was happening until I'd already been stolen from…

The Thief

★

THE THIEF HAD crept in again — not suddenly, but little by little, like the night creeps over the day until finally there's no more light.

I didn't even realize it was happening until I'd already been stolen from — even though I know how thieves work. Most of them will "case" the place they plan to burglarize — for example, watching for weaknesses in a bank's opening or closing procedures, or looking for newspapers piled on the porch of a home whose owners are on vacation. If they notice someone watching them with suspicion or writing down their car license numbers, they will try to pretend they're simply lost. They wait for the right moment to make a surprise attack when the victim is unaware of their presence.

Some thieves go to a home's front door and knock. If someone answers, the thief will ask for someone by name, and then say, "I guess I have the wrong address." If no one answers, the thief tries to find an unlocked door or window, or some other soft spot in the home's defenses. (If easy access can't be found, or if the home has an alarm system, most thieves will leave and try some place else that isn't so well protected.)

Thieves don't want anyone to know who they are, and take steps to avoid it — such as wearing gloves so they won't leave identifying fingerprints.

That's why I'm so amazed my thief was able to sneak in — because I know my thief by name. I've tried to stay on guard for him. I've studied a great deal about him. I've talked with others from whom he has stolen, and they've given me all sorts of advice and precautions. I've tried to be ready for him.

But he seems to know when I'm easy prey. Somehow he manages to slip past all my defenses.

Maybe this same thief has stolen from you too. You may know him by a different name, but I know him as Depression, a vicious intruder bent on stealing all he can get before being caught and driven out.

Depression steals my joy and my sense of self-worth. Depression has at times left me bruised and broken of spirit, driving me down on my knees in a heap of despair that covers me like the darkness of night. Depression's icy fingers rob me of the my strength and my will to continue resisting.

But resist I do...not with my strength, but with the strength of the Savior. Tenderly He comes to me in my darkness. Then He takes and places me, not in the light of day, but in the shadow of the cross, in the same shadow where the centurion stood and proclaimed that the One hanging there was truly the Son of God.

It's the shadow of the same cross on which Jesus carried all my despair, replacing it with the one thing my thief fears even more then being recognized —and that is *hope*.

I read in Psalm 43:5, "Why are you in despair, O my soul? And why are you disturbed within me? Hope in God, for I shall again praise Him..."

★

I tried to reason with him, but it was no use. The scars of hurt and rejection went too deep...

★

Restore the Hearts

★

I COULDN'T WAIT to get out of my police uniform and become a father and husband again.

As I drove up to my house and stopped, I saw the front door fly open and my twelve-year-old daughter Michele burst from it. Right on her heels was Buffy, her cocker spaniel. Both have enthusiasm as if it were meant only for them.

It reminded me how Michele has always eagerly anticipated my homecoming each day. When she was still in diapers, she would crawl up on the bench at our front window about 4:00 P.M. to start watching for her daddy.

As I got out of my car, my mind quickly slipped back to what had happened only an hour earlier...

I'd met with another "daddy" — a dad who asked me to go with him to apprehend his fourteen-year-old son.

It was the same story I'd heard a hundred times, with only the names changed. It started just as they always did: "I can't understand him. He has everything he's ever wanted..."

This dad told me his son was "a good boy — but he just can't get his act together." The father was so exasperated by the disruption in his

*family that he had decided on a drastic measure.
He felt the best thing for everyone was to put the
boy in a boarding school in Idaho, where "they"
would straighten him out. His son would be there
for two years, isolated from friends and family.*

Michele gave me such a huge hug, I thought she
would strangle me. We walked to the front door, her
arm around my waist and mine around hers.

Lotte, my other daughter and two years younger,
was at the front door. She also gave me a big hug,
and wanted to know all about my day. I just couldn't
tell her what had happened that hour before...

*I walked to the door and knocked. The boy who
opened it was surprised to see me. Then he
looked past me, into the face of his dad. I
watched as the boy's face turned red, and the
veins in his neck swelled. He cursed his father
and threatened to kill him if he came near him or
touched him.*

Maggie entered our front hall and joined in the
family hug section. The four of us tried to walk and
hug at the same time, but we fell against the wall
and laughed.

It was so good to be home.

*The boy continued cursing. Whenever the dad
took a step closer, his son would raise his fists
and back away. I tried to reason with him, but it
was no use. The scars of hurt and rejection went
too deep. "He only cares about making money*

and buying cars," he said of his father. "He only cares about himself!"

I asked the dad to wait out by his van while I talked further with the boy. I told him what his dad wanted to do with him. "You don't really have much choice in the matter. You can either go sit in the van and ride peacefully to Idaho, or we'll have to handcuff you to the seat with the handcuffs your dad brought along."

He said he would have to be handcuffed; otherwise he would jump out of the van the first chance he had. He didn't even want to be in the same vehicle as his dad.

I put the handcuffs on him, and we started out the door. When his father came toward us, the boy began screaming and kicking at him.

We finally got him inside the van, and shut the door. The dad got in, thanked me for my help, and started for Idaho. I watched the van drive away. The boy's screams could still be heard until the van turned the corner and disappeared from sight, leaving me standing in silence.

I walked to my police car and reached for my keys. I saw that my hands were trembling as I opened the door.

I slid behind the steering wheel, took in a few breaths, started the engine, and drove away.

At dinner that night, I held each of my daughters' hands as we formed our family circle around the table. As one of the girls prayed, I thought of Malachi 4:6 —"And he will restore the hearts of the fathers to their children, and the hearts of the children to their fathers..."

Dear Jesus, help us fathers.

Help us keep our priorities straight.

Give us courage to resist the world's temptations that

pull us from our families. Restore our hearts to You

so we can restore our hearts to our children.

Amen.

*I stood
by, in case
something went
wrong…*

Missing It

★

FROM INSIDE THE HOUSE we could hear the angry yelling of adults, in language that would have embarrassed the saltiest sailor. I could also hear children crying.

Outside, our police cars had attracted a number of neighborhood kids. One of them said the people who lived there fought all the time.

"You kids go and play now," I suggested. Most of them did, while the rest moved only a short distance away so they could see what was happening.

The other officer knocked on the front door. A woman in her bathrobe opened it. Her face was red and streaked with tears. She asked us to come in. We stepped into the living room where her husband was sitting in a chair, a beer clutched in one hand.

The other officer began talking with them while I stood by, in case something went wrong and we had to arrest someone. Looking around, I saw a large, vividly painted crucifix hanging on the wall.

The husband finally said he would leave for a little while, to cool off. He walked out the door, taking his beer with him. We watched as he walked down the street, and waited until he was around the corner before we got in our police cars and left.

Driving away I thought how incredible it was: Right in their living room was a reminder of the Savior, of His suffering, His sacrifice. Right before them was the answer to their conflict — but they missed it.

I've been in other homes in which couples were arguing about who got what in their divorce settlement, and again, there on the wall, was a crucifix. I've been tempted at times to ask, "Who's going to get the cross?"

Crosses, of course, are not only in our homes. They adorn the steeples and doors and walls of our churches. As jewelry items they hang around our necks or on our key chains. Some gang members even have them tattooed on their arms and chests.

Somehow along the way, we've forgotten what the cross is all about. We've smoothed its rough edges, and taken away any trace of splinters. We've gotten rid of any remaining blood stains. We've turned the cross into something that doesn't offend us or anyone else.

Could it be that we want to disregard the pain suffered there? Maybe we don't want to remember that it was our sin that made the cross necessary in the first place. We want to forget that our own minds invented the cross, and our own hands built it and lifted it into place. And our own voices mocked the One who hung on it. We ourselves secured the cross into the history of mankind.

And yet through that cross God purchased our lives through the death of His Son, Jesus Christ. Our Creator reached down in an instant of time, and changed eternity.

What are you going to do with the cross? You do have a choice, you know.

How often I've gone to homes where children cringed when their father raised his hand...

Hands

★

WE WEREN'T GOING any place special — I think it may have been just a trip to the grocery store. One of my daughters was with me, and we held hands as I drove the short distance.

Just before we arrived, she picked up my hand and gently kissed it. Then she studied it, softly running her own hand back and forth across mine. Then she pressed it against her cheek.

"Daddy," she said, "I really like your hands!"

My daughter liked my hands! I felt a twinge of embarrassment as she held it against her cheek.

Then I began to think how often I've gone as a policeman to homes where children cringed when their father raised his hand, homes where children had been beaten and slapped with hands. And here — my hands were being honored by my daughter!

It reminded me of the responsibility I have for the use of my hands. God made them to serve, and to be lifted up in praise to Him — to serve without limit, and to praise without limit.

I believe that how we use our hands is a direct reflection of our hearts. If our heart is right, we use our hands to do right.

How I would love to study the hands of our Savior...to hold them and examine every line and mark. To be able to softly run my hand over the very hands that made the universe, that created the earth and mankind. To feel the hands of the Physician whose mere touch could heal the sick and raise the dead. To feel the hands that were willingly stretched out on the cross.

And to let my tears of joy fall onto the hands that reached down from that cross and touched me.

*I opened
the card, and
through tears
read the words
in large print…*

Naoma

★

I HARDLY NOTICED the thirteen-year-old girl Maggie was talking to as I looked at the variety of foods brought in for our monthly potluck dinner with families from our church.

Later Maggie rejoined me and said she had met someone who wanted to babysit our girls when we needed a sitter. I looked up from my plate toward the girl as she sat eating by her mother. *She looks awfully young,* I thought. But I trusted Maggie's judgment.

Not long afterward, we phoned and arranged to have her come over while Maggie and I went out. Maggie picked up her, and when she returned they came into the kitchen where I was.

"David," Maggie said, "This is Naoma." Then Maggie disappeared to finish getting ready.

I tried making the usual small talk, and told Naoma to make herself at home. But she seemed so shy I finally just showed her where my daughters were and excused myself and went in the other room.

In the coming months Naoma returned for more babysitting nights, and I was surprised at how freely she talked with Maggie — to the point that I watched to see how long she could go without taking a breath between sentences.

With me, on the other hand, there were always the same awkward silences. Several times when I drove her home, I tried unsuccessfully to engage her in a conversation that required more from her than yes or no answers to my questions. Finally I decided we didn't have anything to talk about, so I made sure Maggie always picked her up and drove her home.

Over time, however, Naoma began talking more freely to me. I even started taking her home on babysitting evenings, and began enjoying our talks.

I knew we had reached a milestone the night I listened to Naoma for the entire trip home without saying a word myself. And she almost did it in only one breath!

From her conversations with us, Maggie and I were gradually getting a picture of Naoma's past. She had been born to "hippie" parents in the late 1960's. Naoma didn't remember her father — he left his family when she was two. Naoma's mother struggled as a single parent, and Naoma seemed to do her best to confuse and frustrate her mother.

When Naoma was nine, her mother decided she needed a break, and sent her to a Christian camp. The week of peace and quiet seemed to go all too quickly, but Naoma returned with the radiant joy that comes only from seeing the Savior. Her mother enjoyed the "new" child in her home, though she didn't understand what was going on, and thought the newness would wear off.

Through special friends and circumstances, Naoma's mother went to church and found herself weeping during the service, not knowing why. Soon afterward she knelt down and placed her life in the

Savior's hand. Now mother and daughter began a new life together.

Maggie and I watched as Naoma and her mother continued growing closer to the Lord and to each other. Naoma was blossoming into a young lady with radiant character.

One night she called to say she would not be able to come over to watch our girls as we had planned. She told us she was sorry, but that she was grounded for a week because she had been disrespectful to her mother — and she said she deserved the punishment. Afterward I thought, *All she had to do was say she couldn't make it* — but Naoma felt we deserved to know the whole story.

We were growing fonder of her as the years went by. We proudly recommended her to a friend of ours who was looking for a reliable Christian teenager to work in his Christian book store. It was great to walk into the store and be met with a hug and a smile from such a special girl.

Naoma began house-sitting for us when Maggie and I had ministry trips out of town. I even gave her the keys to my car, which I never lend out to anyone. But Naoma wasn't just anyone — she was "family."

The high school years went quickly by and suddenly Naoma was to graduate. At the ceremony, we could see Naoma and her mother communicating through smiles and waves. I felt I was watching a true miracle of the Lord. I thought of the hurdles both Naoma and her mother had overcome, and what an encouraging example Naoma's mother is to other single parents.

Naoma planned to begin attending a Christian college in California the following fall. That summer

she worked as many hours as possible at the book-
store, making money to help ease the burden of college expenses on her mother.

Too quickly the summer was over. Naoma's
mother gave her a going-away dinner to celebrate
this giant step into the future. We laughed a lot, and
had a great time looking at old pictures of Naoma
and her "hippie" mother. We took snapshots of each
other, and I was honored when Naoma wanted a picture of just her and me. Sharing that special evening
together, we found it hard to leave. We hugged and
said our goodbys, promised to phone and write, then
went home.

We received our first letter from her a few days
later. I wrote back and added a postscript: "If you
ever need a substitute Dad, I would like to volunteer
for the position."

A few days later I received in the mail a large envelope. It was a card from Naoma. I opened it, and
through tears read the words in large print: "I love
you Dad."

Someday, perhaps I'll be in a church pew, watching a young woman walk down the aisle to be married, and I'll think of her story. Again I'll be in awe of
the Heavenly Father, who watches over His children.
And I'll weep with joy.

*I thought how
this present
Christmas would
soon be another
past Christmas...*

What Memories!

★

OUR HOUSE WAS DECORATED for Christmas. Sitting in the living room, listening to carols on the radio, I began looking at all the little Christmas items Maggie and I had collected over our years of marriage, and it brought a flood of memories.

On our mantle was a little Dickens-era village we bought while on vacation in Williamsburg, Virginia. We saw it in a shop window, and Maggie described how wonderful it would look over the fireplace — while I wondered how we could pay for it and how we could get it home on the airplane. As usual, Maggie was able to dispel my worries, and we got it. I'm glad we did...now it brings back to mind that special vacation together.

Above the village was a huge wreath. A smaller one used to hang there, but Maggie said she wanted a larger one. One evening while we were in shopping mall mall where the girls were to appear in a choir performance, I sneaked away and bought it. We got home and I opened the trunk of the car and pulled it out. As Maggie often does when I surprise her like that, she slugged me in the arm and said I was a big softy. Call it romance.

All over the living room were candles — red and green, big and little, scented and unscented, short and tall. Maggie likes having candles burn all the time in our house. She loves the soft glow and the warmth they project. I worry about the smoke detector going off, and wax dripping onto the rugs or furniture. But that evening their sight and smell reminded me of our trips together to the candle factory at Half Moon Bay, not far from our home. We like to go there early in the morning so we can beat the crowds to the bargains in the "seconds" shop. Then we load the boxes of candles into the car and drive to a restaurant overlooking the Pacific, and use all the money we saved at the candle shop to have lunch together.

I almost hated to see the candles burn, fearing that when they were gone, the memories would be gone too. But I remembered that the factory is only a short drive away; and besides, I really liked the clam chowder at our special restaurant.

I soaked in the sight of the Christmas books laying on the table, and the ceramic creche that Maggie's grandmother made.

And then, of course, there was our Christmas tree. Each ornament had a story all its own; but it hadn't always been that way. When we were first married, we decorated our tree with the plain colored balls and tinsel. Then over the years we replaced them with special ornaments that we or the girls bought or made.

On top of the tree was our special Christmas star. Maggie's dad made it for us the first year we were married, when we didn't have lots of money to spend on frills. He crafted it out of a coat-hanger and gold garland, with a place in the center for a Christmas light bulb. It's a treasure not only because of who made it, but also because it rekindles the memories of our newlywed days, when we struggled to make ends meet.

Around the base of our tree was my "toy." We

bought it for the girls years ago when they were small, but they never quite got ownership of it. So it's always been referred to as "Daddy's train" — a large-gauge set made in Germany. Maggie and I found it when we were in Carmel for a getaway weekend. I could still see Maggie's face as I tried with the most sincere look to convince her our daughters would love it. So we bought it "for the children."

A thousand memories danced through my head that night. And I thought how this present Christmas would soon be another past Christmas. On Christmas Eve we would again read and hear together the Christmas story from the gospel of Luke. In spite of what the world has done to take Christ out of Christmas, to change it into merely a time for "good feelings" for one another, we and others like us all over the world would stop and retell that wondrous story — how Mary and Joseph went to Bethlehem, and there the Creator of the universe became flesh, in the form of a baby born in a stable. Their children will have it in their memories, and will pass it on to their children, who will pass it on again.

Finally the day will come when Jesus returns. Then, from His memory, He will call His own together — and we'll celebrate Christmas for eternity.

*She paused,
and said, 'You
knew I was lying,
didn't you?'*

The Apology

★

AT WORK THAT MORNING I opened the folder containing my time sheet, court notices, and other communications. Flipping through them, I saw a telephone message requesting me to call a woman whose name I didn't recognize. There was no indication of the nature of the call.

I dislike notes like that. In most cases they're from people who want to complain about a ticket they received, or about a traffic accident for which the other person won't pay damages, and they want me to "make him pay." I usually have to listen to a complete description of the accident and their problem with the insurance companies and their problem with the judicial system. Sometimes people just want someone to listen to their story. At other times they only want to yell at somebody, and I guess they figure a police officer is as good a person to yell at as anyone. I've even had people yell at me and then hang up before I could find out what they were upset about.

I continued going through other pieces of information in my folder, and found another phone message from the same woman — and then another. I looked at the dates: She had called on my days off. I tucked the notes in my shirt pocket and decided I would phone her sometime later in my shift, since it was then only 6:30 A.M.

The day turned out to be a busy one. As I was driving my police car back to headquarters, I remembered the messages and decided I would phone her when I got off duty. But while winding my way through traffic, I heard my unit number called on the radio, and I was told I had a phone number to call. I pulled over to the side of the road so I could write it down. The radio operator began by giving the name of the person to call — and I recognized it as the woman whose messages I had in my pocket.

At headquarters I turned in my car and shotgun to the supply clerk, then headed to the report-writing room, which has several telephones. I dialed the number. It rang once and then was picked up. The woman identified herself. When I said who I was, she told me how glad she was that I called, then began updating me on a long list of concerns — her financial problems, the mental breakdown she had suffered a month earlier, an automobile accident she had on Thanksgiving night while trying to deliver a dinner to a needy family, a trial she had been involved in, and her marital problems.

Finally I was able to interrupt her. "I'm sorry," I told her, "but I just don't have the slightest idea what you're talking about."

There was a moment of silence. Then she said, "You don't remember me?"

"I'm sorry," I said again, "but your name just doesn't ring a bell."

She then reminded me that I had arrested her at a local drug store for forging a prescription. I told her I remembered the case, then asked what I could do for her.

"I want to apologize to you," she said. "I lied to you when I told you I wasn't the one who wrote the

name on that prescription. I didn't think it would
hurt to lie to a police officer, since the police were
only investigating the case and wouldn't be losing
anything if I lied. But afterwards I felt bad about it.

"You were so nice to me," she said, "even after
you arrested me. You loosened the handcuffs when I
said they were too tight, and when I told you I was
freaking out when I had to wait in that cramped
back seat of your car, you opened the door and let
me put my legs out."

She recalled that I had bent down to her when I
talked with her, and, more importantly, I had listened to her, even though she was lying.

Then she paused, and said, "You knew I was
lying, didn't you?"

I told her I had suspected she was, because of
the inconsistencies in her story.

"I knew that — and still you were so nice to me.
And during the entire investigation, you were the
only one who cared enough to try to find out why I
was trying to get the drugs."

The woman again related some of the recent
troubles she had suffered, and asked my opinion on
what I thought she should do. Finally she said that
she would let me go, and thanked me again for calling her back and for accepting her apology.

After hanging up the phone, I thought of the
apostle Paul's words in his letter to the Colossians:
"*Whatever you do* in word or deed, do all in the name
of the Lord Jesus" (3:17). I think Paul would say this
command applies even to arresting a drug prescription forgerer.

We never know whose lives are waiting to be

touched by our everyday activities. As God's word teaches, we simply need to be walking with Him every day, letting our words and actions be a reflection of the One with whom we walk.

*I glanced back
at the money
she left on
the table…*

Counting the Cost

★

I'D BEEN CAMPING OUT in the book of Luke for a while in my daily Bible reading, and trying to put what I had read into practical everyday application. But it was depressing now as I drove to work, thinking about the verses I'd read that morning in Luke 14. Especially the last verse in the passage — "He who has ears to hear, let him hear"; all I could hear was the guy in the car behind me honking his horn, because the traffic light had changed to green and I wasn't moving.

I knew today's verses were important, or else they wouldn't have been included in the Bible. (Sometimes I amaze myself with profound conclusions like that.) But now my mind drew a blank, as I searched for something to help the passage come alive.

I arrived at work, and my mind shifted into the police mode. I began my routine of preparing to go out on patrol — making sure I had all the forms I needed, and making sure the car that I'd call my "office" for the next ten hours was ready.

As I started driving toward my beat, my police radio informed me that there was a burglary alarm sounding at a business. The dispatcher asked if I wanted another officer to respond with me. I said I didn't think that would be necessary, because false alarms had sounded at the same address each of the last few mornings.

I arrived, checked out the building, and found it to be another false alarm. The business owner arrived, and apologized that I'd had to respond again. I filled out the appropriate form, and handed it to him, explaining that he would more than likely be charged for the police response. (The police department had begun charging fines to any address having two false alarms that we respond to in any sixty-day period; we found that when business owners find that false alarms will cost them something, they usually get the alarm fixed.)

"Do you know how much the fine will be?" he asked.

"Somewhere between a hundred and fifty and two hundred dollars, " I answered.

He turned to walk away, and said, "I'm going to call the alarm company right now. It would have been cheaper if I'd have called them when I first began having this trouble."

I went back into service, and another officer radioed to see if I could have coffee with him. There were no calls waiting, so I met with him at a little breakfast shop called "Our Daily Bread." We bought our coffee, and sat down. I could see something was bothering him, and asked what it was.

"Do you know how much it costs to send a child to college?" he began.

Not having a college-age child yet, I didn't know the answer. He told me he would have to take a second mortgage out on his house to help pay not only for his daughter's college education, but for her car too.

We talked a while longer about college costs, and it made me think that I needed to plan now for that future expense. I knew it was going to cost plenty by the time my daughters were ready for college (though I hope the Rapture will come first, and save me from that tribulation).

We finished our coffee and went back on patrol.

A short time later, I stopped a driver who had just run a red light. She was very apologetic, and said she was in a hurry to get to an appointment. I gave her a ticket.

"How much will it cost?" she asked. I told her I didn't know, as I handed her copy to her.

She looked at the ticket and said, "I guess I should have left earlier. I'm late for my appointment, I have a fine — and my insurance rate will probably go up."

Toward the end of the day I was assigned a call to accompany officials from the county licensing department on a visit to a day care center in a home. They told me they were investigating a complaint from one of the children's parents.

We entered the home and I sat and listened as the license investigator asked questions. I began looking into the next room at the children, who were lying down to take naps. One of them began to cry softly for his mother, and an older child tried to comfort him. "It's all right, " he said, pulling the child's blanket over him.

I thought about the mothers and fathers who day after day drop their children off to be raised by someone else. What compels them to make that kind of choice? Oh, I know what many will say: "We have to pay for a nice home, " or "I'm divorced and have to work," or "My career is important—besides, I still spend *quality* time with my child." But that crying child's quality time with a parent had just been lost when he called for a mother who wasn't there.

As the licensing people were looking through a file, a check fell out and landed face down on the floor next to my feet. I picked it up and handed it back. As I did, I wondered how much it cost to have these children in day care — and what will be the cost in the future to a society that "farms out" its children, then wonders why they rebel against our values?

I left the day care home and drove back to "Our Daily Bread" to write my report. While I was writing, a mother and her preschool daughter came in and sat down, ordering soft drinks and rolls. The little girl had on a pink dress and patent leather shoes — she was "cute as a button." As I wrote, I glanced up from time to time and watched them as they talked and laughed together.

Soon their waitress stepped to their table and handed the women her check. The women left the money on the table, then she and her daughter walked out of the restaurant holding hands.

I glanced back at the money she left on the table — and I suddenly realized the everyday application the Lord had been showing me for that day's passage, and specifically verse 28: "For which one of you, when he wants to build a tower, does not first sit down and calculate the cost, to see if he has enough to complete it?" All day long the Lord had been trying to get me to "hear" that — through the man with the faulty alarm, my fellow officer who had failed to plan for his daughter's college costs, the woman who was ticketed for running a red light, and the parents who were failing to count the costs of leaving their children in day care.

Here in the restaurant, however, I had witnessed a mother who had counted the cost — and found that it wasn't too high.

*He was like
a diamond
that God had
been carefully
chipping and
polishing for
ninety years…*

Landmarks

★

I HAD JUST FINISHED straightening the stacks of brochures on the table. I picked up a book that I'd brought along to read during slow times like this. The people attending the Sunday school convention were now in another workshop session, leaving the exhibit area nearly deserted until the next break, when they would again swarm to our booth and the others around me.

As I seated myself I noticed an older gentleman walking toward me. I set down my book, and stood up just as he reached the booth. I extended my hand and introduced myself to him. His hand was frail, but he still possessed a strong grip.

He introduced himself as Mr. Townsend, then asked what I was promoting. I told him about the Family Life Conferences sponsored by the Family Ministry of Campus Crusade for Christ. Maggie and I had attended our first such conference ten years earlier. It had changed our lives, and also given us a burden for the lives of other families.

Mr. Townsend picked up a brochure and began to thumb through its pages. Finally he placed it back onto one of the stacks, and tenderly straightened it. Then he looked at me and said he thought the conference was a good idea.

We talked for a while, then I invited him to sit in

the booth with me. He accepted, and came in. His steps were slow and deliberate as he moved to the chair and sat down.

We carried on small talk, and I asked his age. With great pride he told me that he had just passed his ninetieth birthday. Reaching into his coat pocket, he pulled out a copy of a letter he had written on his birthday and sent to his friends. I unfolded it and began to read.

In it he reflected on a life of blessings, and on what he believed was truly important in life. He said he now soaks in "the sunrises and sunsets, the birds singing, and the rolling clouds." He thanked God for his wife — "the most beautiful girl in the world" — and for the special friends he had known through the years. He spoke of his dreams about what might have been, but said he knew his dream of eternity with the Father was "now nearer than ever before."

He referred to his ninetieth birthday as "a landmark," and said he knew it was time to start saying his goodbys to those who had loved him and whom he had loved. "Being loved and giving love," he wrote in his concluding line, "is what life is all about." The letter was signed simply with his name.

I refolded the letter, and asked if I could keep this copy.

"I only give them to my friends," he said with a smile. "So you can keep it."

We talked for a while longer. I have always enjoyed hearing the elderly tell of their lives, their hopes, and their dreams — and now again I was reminded of the wealth of knowledge that the elderly possess, a wealth that we as a nation are neglecting.

I was reminded too that some of the elderly are neglecting that treasure themselves. As a police officer, I have seen many who had resigned themselves to sit and watch life go by. I know that many older people are physically unable to do much more in life; but I also know of others who seem to have simply given up.

As all of us do, they reached landmarks in life, events that confronted them with a choice: to either continue pressing forward on the road before them, or to simply stop, and turn their backs on the future. As a police officer, all too often I had seen those who had chosen to give up on life. For some reason known only to themselves, they let a landmark become a roadblock instead of guide. Something had taken away their spark of really living as God planned them to.

Mr. Townsend had reached a landmark — and had paused to give thanks and to find God's guidance and direction as he continued down the path of life. And he warmed me with his spark of his life.

Soon the convention workshops ended and the crowds approached. Mr. Townsend got up and slowly walked into the now swelling wave of people. I tucked his letter into my coat pocket as he disappeared from sight.

I suddenly realized I had been talking with a living Proverb. I picked up a Bible and turned to Proverbs 20:29 — "The glory of young men is their strength, and the honor of old men is their gray hair." I knew Mr. Townsend was one of the old men those words were referring to, a man to be honored.

Our meeting was for only a few moments, but in those moments God showed me that Erwin Townsend was like a diamond that He had been carefully chipping and polishing for ninety years...and now He had allowed me to see the nearly finished gem, sparkling its radiance onto my life.

'If you ever
go through a
divorce,' he said,
'I don't even
want to hear
about it.'

Placing Our Faith

★

I WALKED INTO the firehouse kitchen with my usual greeting: "Don't get up, it's only me."

I normally take my lunch to work, and the fire station on my beat makes a nice place where I can relax and enjoy it, as well as get to know the firefighters there. Besides, one of them is a great cook, and from time to time he "forces" me to eat his great soups and potato salad.

A fireman named Gary looked up and said, "Hi, O. J." (my nickname there, for Officer Johnson).

I could tell something was wrong. There weren't the usual smiles in the crew's faces. I looked around the room and realized someone was missing.

"Gary, where's Ted?"

"He called in a sick day."

"I hope it's nothing serious."

Gary looked at me through eyes of pain, and said in a low voice, "He's not sick — his wife told him last night she was leaving him."

I could hardly believe his words. Ted had been married for twenty-five years, and none of us suspected anything was wrong in their marriage.

I called Ted's home, and assured him I was as close as his phone if he needed anything. I could tell by his voice that he wasn't angry — just deeply hurt. We talked a while longer, then I handed the phone to Gary. I stood there watching and listening to the pain being shared by two close friends. Gary himself had gone through a divorce a year earlier. I felt sure the pain he had suffered was surfacing again.

Gary hung the phone up and just shook his head. "I just can't believe it. Next to you, O. J., Ted had what I thought was one of the strongest marriages around."

I hadn't realized how much Gary had observed my marriage. Gary had met Maggie and my daughters only once, when they came to the firehouse with a group of children and mothers for a tour. He later commented on what a "neat" family I had, and how lucky I was to have a wife like Maggie. (I'd already told him that, but I guess he had to meet her before he could believe she was all I had said she was.)

We talked a while longer, then I had to go back on duty. As I headed out of the station, Gary came to me and said, "O. J., if you ever go through this, I'll lose all faith in marriage. As a matter of fact, if you ever go through a divorce, I don't even want to hear about it."

Driving away from the firehouse, I thought of Maggie, and I praised God and thanked Him for blessing me with a wife who was not only a wonderful mate, but a fantastic mother to my children, my best friend, and my GREAT lover!

And I thought about the foundation on which our marriage was built. When we were first married, we knew that only the presence of Christ in our relationship would allow us to weather all the storms coming our way during our life together. God, who laid the foundation for the universe and the world, laid the right foundation for our marriage as well.

I remembered the times at the fire station when I explained gently to Gary and Ted that Jesus was the reason my marriage with Maggie was strong and secure. But I could tell they weren't interested in a "religious" security for their families. I felt frustrated, because I felt they'd bought into what the world offered as the key to happiness.

That lunchtime reaffirmed for me why, for the past ten years, Maggie and I have dedicated our lives to helping families build their foundation on Christ. We're convinced that the strength of America rests on the strength of the family unit. We hold the torch high, so other families might see the way to the One who holds marriages together.

It isn't an easy task. Our arms get tired holding up the flame, and our grip begins to slip. Then we turn our hearts back to God's word — "So take a new grip with your tired hands, stand firm on your shaky legs, and mark out a straight, smooth path for your feet so that those who follow you, though weak and lame, will not fall and hurt themselves, but become strong" (Hebrews 12:12, *The Living Bible*).

*I told her that
never before in
my entire life had
I received such
clear direction…*

A Story I Must Tell

★

September 20, 1974. Hurricane Fifi, one of the largest storms of the century, hovered off the coast of Honduras. At about 2:00 A.M. the storm unexpectedly changed direction and crashed into the country's northern tip — bringing with it death to nearly ten thousand people and leaving 350,000 homeless. Damage was estimated at a half billion dollars. In a few hours, Fifi had literally changed the lives of thousands of unsuspecting people.

Among them, two thousand miles away, was a 27-year-old policeman asleep in his bed — and unaware that God was about to tap him on the shoulder and call his name.

Just seven weeks earlier, God had performed a miracle when Maggie gave birth to our first child, Michele. The doctors had said we would never be able to have children, and we tried everything humanly possible before we finally poured out our hearts to the Lord. Now we had a healthy daughter who was the joy of our lives. We told anyone who would listen what God had done. Needless to say, it was a faith-building experience for both of us.

(It wasn't the first time God had performed a miracle for us. A few years earlier when I applied to be a policeman, I was told I couldn't qualify because of a

past back injury in an automobile accident. It was a
crushing blow because this had been my life's ambition since childhood, and I had majored in law enforcement in college in anticipation of a career as a
policeman. God intervened — and following a hearing before the Civil Service Commission, I was hired
by the San Jose Police Department.)

On the Sunday evening after the hurricane
struck Honduras, I was helping another Christian
police officer, Tim Jones, to control traffic outside
our church. We had volunteered for this regular duty
when our church's fast growth led to complaints
from neighbors about the increase in traffic.

When we had finished our traffic control duties,
we walked into the evening service just before our
newly arrived youth pastor, Dave Coursen, stood up
before the congregation. Dave said that several
months earlier he and his wife and a busload of high
school students had worked with a missionary in the
Honduran town of La Ceiba. Now, since the hurricane, no word had been received about whether the
missionary and his family was dead or alive.

Dave added that, on the day before, he had been
contacted by a friend from Seattle who felt led by
God to get relief to the stricken area. The Lord had
supplied more than a ton of medical supplies and
food for the relief effort. Dave said that he, along
with a doctor and some college students, were leaving the next morning to go to Honduras. He asked
for prayer for their safety and for provision of their financial needs.

Dave stepped down from the platform and sat
down in the audience with his wife. Our senior
pastor stood and prayed for the team that was going,
then suggested taking a special collection to help

pay for the trip. After the collection was taken, the pastor began his message.

I sat there trying to concentrate on the sermon, but God was trying to give me another message. It was as if He were tapping me on the shoulder and whispering to me the words of Isaiah 6:8 — "Then I heard the voice of the Lord saying, 'Whom shall I send, and who will go for Us?' Then I said, 'Here am I. Send me!' "

I tried to tell myself that I was being caught up in the emotion of the evening, but the voice persisted. I kept asking myself what good I could do in Honduras. Besides, I was the father of a seven-week old daughter — what would happen to her and Maggie if something happened to me?

I had valid reasons for not going. Yet God kept calling me by name.

When the service was nearly over, Tim and I left early to get to our traffic control positions. We found that we had left a little earlier then we needed to, so we sat in Tim's car and talked for a while. I decided to tell Tim what I was feeling. Without hesitation, he said that if God was calling me to go, I had better obey His call and go!

We finished directing traffic and went back inside to meet our wives. I told Maggie that I needed to check on something, and would be right back. As I walked to Dave's office, I prayed that God would make it perfectly clear what He had in mind for me.

I found Dave and told him that I felt God was calling me to go with the team to Honduras. He, too, said that if God was calling me to go, I should go. I picked up his phone and called the police department. I figured that if God really wanted me to go He would give me the time off from work. I would be asking for the entire week off at the last minute, and the chances of that happening were not very good.

My call was answered by the lieutenant in charge of our shift, rather than the patrol officer who regularly handles the phones. I recognized his voice, and knew that he was a fellow believer. I told him my story. When I finished he said, "If God is calling you to go to Honduras, you'd better go." I was beginning to get the message loud and clear.

I hung up the phone and told Dave I would see him in the morning. As I started out, I turned and asked, "How are we going anyway?"

Dave only smiled and said, "I don't know. I'm praying about that right now."

I walked back to where I had left Maggie and Michele. Maggie just looked at me and said, "You're going to Honduras, aren't you?"

"Yes," I told her.

"I knew it," she replied.

I told her what had happened during the service and, and then afterward with Tim, Dave, and the police lieutenant. I told her that never before in my entire life had I received such clear direction.

We drove home, and I began preparing for the trip. When we went to bed, Maggie and I prayed for God's will to be done during the trip. As I went to sleep I wondered what my next few days would be like. I was going to be in a strange country where people spoke a different language and had different customs, a country which had just suffered a devastating disaster. I wondered what God had in store for me.

Meanwhile Dave Coursen had driven to nearby San Jose Airport. He asked God to direct him to an airplane. He went and stood before an old twin-engine DC-3. On its tail was painted an obviously drunk duck wearing flight goggles and holding a beer bottle. Dave took down the plane's identification number, and from that found out that it was a former cargo plane refurbished as a pleasure craft. It was owned by a group of twenty-three doctors and lawyers. The first name on the owners' list was a dentist. Dave phoned him and introduced himself. He told this perfect stranger that God had directed him to their airplane, and that God wanted to use it to fly food, clothing, and medical supplies to Honduras. After talking with the dentist for fifteen minutes, he said we could use the plane on one condition: That he be allowed to go along as co-pilot.

God was again supplying our needs. Up to that moment we had a pilot, but no co-pilot — now, we had both.

On Monday morning we all arrived at the church, then drove to the airport. We discovered that because of the airplane's design, we couldn't take the clothing and food if we were going to take the people. Dave called us all together, and we did what I thought, at the time, was a little strange: We all prayed about it! I believed in the power of prayer, but I thought we would at least discuss the pros and cons of the situation. God was beginning to teach me about the absolute power of prayer.

After about thirty minutes of praying, it seemed clear that God wanted us to go, and that arrangements for the delivery of the food and clothing would be made later. So we loaded the plane with our personal gear, then filled all the other available space with medical supplies.

One of the pastors going along had been given responsibility for getting food for us from the donated supply. After being in the air for a couple of hours, we began to examine what he picked out for us: Along with some packets of buffalo jerky, there were cans and cans of sardines — and nothing else. He couldn't understand why everyone was so upset, thinking we all liked sardines as much as he did. (By the end of the trip, even he didn't care for them that much.)

The first leg of our journey took us to a refueling stop in New Mexico. We then flew to Brownsville, Texas, where we decided to spend the night because it was getting dark. The airport was small, and the airport director told us we could sleep in the terminal, which would be closed and locked at 11:00 P.M. We spent a rich time in prayer together before going to sleep.

We were all in the plane by 7:00 A.M. Tuesday, ready to get to Honduras and be about the Lord's work. The pilot started the engines and began to taxi down the air strip. Suddenly one of the engines began to backfire, and then stopped. He restarted the engine, and once again it backfired and stopped. Finally, we taxied back to the air terminal, where we had to contact a mechanic. We waited for an hour while he worked on the engine. Several members of our group talked with the mechanic, and after he heard our story, he didn't charge us for his labor. Soon we were airborne again.

Our next stop was Vera Cruz, Mexico. As we taxied toward the airport terminal there, we saw a jeep full of armed soldiers driving out to meet the plane. When we got out, we were told not to leave the area. An official "hold" had been placed on the plane, which meant a delay of at least four hours while the the plane was searched. I couldn't understand what

God was trying to do! We needed to get to Honduras!
There were people waiting for our medical supplies.

We decided we needed to pray. We all gathered
under the tail section of the plane, away from the
glare of the hot sun, and prayed that God would
direct the officials to release the plane. As we finished praying, the government official came out and
told us the hold had been lifted and we could get our
plane refueled and be on our way. We thanked God,
and began refueling the plane. Just as we were finishing, we saw another DC-3 coming in for a landing. On its tail was a large white cross. It was a relief
plane from Seattle on the way to Honduras. We met
with the pilot and co-pilot for a few moments of
Christian fellowship. The government official informed their pilot that no hold would be put on their
plane, and they could refuel and leave when they
wanted.

The plane from Seattle was loaded with supplies,
but they didn't have anyone to distribute them. Our
plane had men, but not many supplies. Both were
headed for the same airport in Honduras. It wasn't
difficult to see that God had this all planned. As His
word declares in Proverbs 16:9, "The mind of man
plans his way, but the Lord directs his steps."

As our plane lifted from the runway, we all knew
that, with God's help, our next stop would be La
Ceiba, Honduras.

As we flew south, we could see large thunder-
heads, leftovers from Hurricane Fifi. The clouds were
moving north, as if searching for who to challenge
next. The plane seemed like a small insect next to
them. I prayed that we wouldn't be their next
victim.

With several hours to go, we gathered together
and prayed. Then we all settled back in our seats —

some slept, while others talked or stared out the window alone with their thoughts.

The further south we flew, the less threatening were the clouds we encountered. As we came over Honduras, the skies were for the most part clear. Near the hardest hit areas we noticed huge columns of smoke drifting up from the villages below. We later learned that the fires were massive funeral fires — the bodies could not be buried fast enough to prevent disease from spreading.

As we continued to fly over the miles and miles of the storm-wrecked country, the reality of the disaster began to sink in. The plane fell silent except for an occasional word of disbelief as we all stared at the scene below.

Our co-pilot leaned out of the open doorway of the cockpit and announced that the La Ceiba airport was directly ahead. He then turned his attention back to the plane's radio and began talking to the airport tower. He was told that they wouldn't give us clearance to land until they knew who we were, and what country we represented. The co-pilot tried to explain who we were, but seemed to have little success.

Finally, in complete frustration, he took off his head phones and said to the pilot, "Let's just circle the airport and land!"

We began making a wide circle, and as we did the pilot noticed an American C-130 transport airplane that was also circling. We fell in behind it, and landed just after it did.

As we taxied off the runway, we were met this time by three trucks full of armed soldiers! They jumped out of the trucks and surrounded the plane.

I thought it seemed just like in the movies.

We opened the door and assured the military personnel that we were friendly, and that we had medical supplies on board. One of the soldiers came into the plane and, after looking around, got off and reported that we indeed had medical supplies on board. I was hoping they would confiscate the sardines and buffalo jerky, but they didn't seem interested in them. After chastising us for landing without proper clearance, the soldiers got back into the trucks and left.

Two civilians — one a younger man, and one

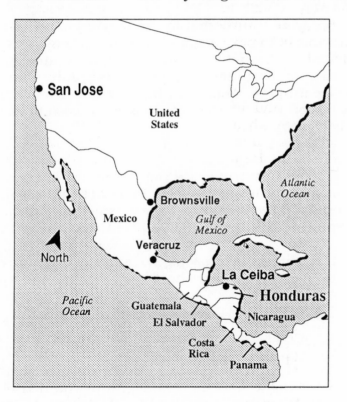

older — walked up to the plane and spoke in Spanish to Dave for a few minutes. They were father and
son. The father began pounding on the son's shoulder in a good-natured way. He had a big grin on his
face.

Dave stepped back into the plane and said to us,
"You're not going to believe this, but the man owns
one of the major hotels in the city which wasn't hurt
by the hurricane and he wants us to stay there at no
charge!" Dave added that the man's son had always
been critical of Americans. His dad had told him that
one day he would have to "eat" his words. That day
had just arrived!

We were transported to the hotel by hotel cabs,
and shown to our comfortable rooms. Then we were
invited to the hotel's restaurant and treated to a
great Honduran dinner (no sardines!). After dinner
we went to our rooms and had our first showers in
two days. Then we went to sleep. It felt good to be in
a bed again.

The next morning we rose early and ate some
fruit that the hotel owner left in baskets outside our
rooms. Dave telephoned the missionary we had
wanted to check on, and learned that the entire
family was safe. The husband had gone out in the
countryside to help people recover from the hurricane and hadn't come home yet, but no one was
worried.

We then headed back to the airport. Part of our
group would need air transportation to other areas
of the country. At the airport we split into three
groups. One group was to go to the Roatan Islands
just off the coast. A second group would travel
inland toward the west, and the last group — the
group I was in — was going south to the Rio Agua

Valley. My group included a doctor, two college students and myself.

Transportation would be no problem for us, since the United States had flown planes and helicopters to Honduras to help in the relief. All we needed to do was ask, and the military would fly us wherever we wanted to go. We boarded a government-owned DC-3 and headed for the Rio Agua Valley, only thirty minutes away.

Unlike the plane we flew in earlier, this one was stripped to the walls. We sat on the floor among the medical supplies we had brought. When we neared the crude landing strip, the pilot warned us that the landing might be a little rough. We hit the grass airfield with a hard thump and bounced into the air. When we finally landed and taxied in, I looked out the window and saw, to my horror, the wreckage of several planes on the side of the runway.

We got out and unloaded our boxes of medical supplies. When all was unloaded, the plane pulled to the end of the runway. We watched as the pilot struggled with the controls as he attempted to take off from the grassy ground that seemed to grab at the plane's wheels in an attempt to claim another victim. Finally after what seemed like an eternity, the wheels finally slipped from the grass and the plane was airborne. I realized that I had been holding my breath, so I took in a gulp of air and relaxed my body.

As I looked around the area, I couldn't believe such poverty existed. The few homes still standing nearby were made of mud, grass, and corrugated sheets of metal for the roof. The roads were dirt; it appeared that cars rarely, if ever, used them. I felt as if I had stepped back in time. There were no electri-

★

cal poles in sight. Gutters and sewers were nonexistent as well.

We picked up the boxes and started walking towards a little village about a half mile from the airfield. We asked for directions to the village's medical office, and one of the villagers took us down a side street to a mud hut. About sixty or seventy people were waiting outside in a line, each with an injury of some kind.

The four of us made our way to the door and went inside. The interior was dark, the only light coming from a glass kerosene lantern. The doctor introduced himself to the village doctor and told him why we were there. We showed him the medical supplies and started unloading them in the office. We decided that the doctor and I would assist the village doctor there, while the other two members of our group would travel to another village two miles away to see if they could help out there.

As a Marine Corps recruit back in 1968, I had been instructed to label my fatigues with my first and second initial along with my last name. My name therefore appeared to read DR JOHNSON. I was wearing those fatigues now, and although most of the villagers in that little medical clinic could not read English, I suppose they figured out that since their doctor had a DR before his name, I must be a doctor as well! I was asked by the clinic's doctor to treat the wounded and to give necessary penicillin injections.

We did the best that we could with what we had, and that was all that we could do. Because of the delays on the way down from the United States, our time in Honduras was all too short. Soon it was time to leave and catch a flight back to La Ceiba. We were to meet back at the airport and spend the night on the plane, then fly out of Honduras at 7:30 A.M. By leaving that early we could reach the United States by nightfall — we could spend the night in Texas and fly the rest of the way the next day, which was Sunday. Awaiting us at home were pressing matters. The doctor was scheduled to be in the emergency room at his hospital on Monday, while I was to fly to Portland, Oregon to testify in federal court — I was a key figure in the prosecution of four individuals charged with armed robbery of four banks and the bombing of several government buildings.

The doctor and I walked back to the airport and located a military radio man. He told us that a helicopter had just left and was to return after refueling and dropping off supplies. It would more than likely be a little more than an hour before it could return and pick us up for our return flight back to La Ceiba. I settled down on the edge of the airstrip to wait for the helicopter to return. The gentle westerly breeze that blew down the lush green valley felt cool against my face

Then I heard a slight commotion in a nearby corral. I got up and walked over, and watched as a villager helped deliver some little piglets. As each one was born, the villagers standing around would cheer. It felt good to see new life being born in the midst of so much death. It took more than an hour for the sow to deliver all her babies, but finally she was through, and then she just lay there nursing her newborns.

As I turned to walk back to where the doctor was napping, I looked to the west, up the valley. While I was enjoying the birth of the baby pigs, a weather front had appeared and was now moving towards us. I walked to the radio man's position and commented about the approaching rain. He said he had been watching it for a while, and that it was moving towards us quite rapidly. He said he had talked by radio with the helicopter, and it was on its way to pick us up.

He continued talking on the radio, then took off his headphones, unplugged them from the radio, and began to dismantle the radio set. He looked at me and said the helicopter pilot saw the storm and was turning around and heading back to La Ceiba. They wouldn't return here until 10:30 A.M. By then, I knew our plane home would have already left. We knew they couldn't wait for the two of us — we had all agreed that any of us who didn't make it back to the plane in time would have to find their own transportation back home.

I ran to where the doctor was sleeping, woke him up, and told him the news. We both stood there staring at the wall of advancing rain that was now only a half mile away.

From the corner of my mind, the words in Matthew 21:22 echoed in my ear: "And all things you ask in prayer, believing, you shall receive." Prayer had been the theme of our entire trip. God had answered all our prayers. He had waited for us to call upon Him, and then took care of us, His children.

And so, as we had done so many times before on that trip, we knelt down there on the airfield and prayed. We reminded God that we needed to be back to the plane by morning, and that they wouldn't wait for us. We ended by thanking Him for watching over us and for doing all that He had done for us.

We finished and stood up as we felt the first few drops of rain strike our faces. The torrent had advanced to the end of the airstrip and was now about to envelope us. Suddenly, as if it had run into a giant, invisible barrier, the advancing rain stopped. The clouds began to spread out and then encircle the airstrip. The rain was now falling on all four sides of the airfield, yet only a light drizzle landed on us. Overhead was a circle of blue sky, with not a cloud in it.

Suddenly in the opening a helicopter appeared. It dropped straight down and landed in front of us. I could see the pilots waving for us to come and get on board. We ran to the aircraft and jumped in. As soon as we were inside, the helicopter lifted off the ground and headed straight up. One of the crew members handed each of us a flight helmet which was equipped with a microphone. We continued to rise and finally we flew up through the hole in the clouds. As we cleared the clouds, the hole closed in and swallowed the opening so that all we could see was a solid cloud cover. Chills shot up my back, as the reality of what had happened overtook me. I was sure I felt as the children of Israel must have felt when God parted the sea for them, and then closed it on the Egyptians.

The pilot said that he had almost decided to head back when he saw the opening in the clouds. He said he didn't know why, but he decided to fly over it to see what was causing the hole. When he saw us, he decided to go ahead and try to pick us up. He said he had never seen anything like it. I told the pilot that the doctor and I had prayed and that God had answered our prayers. The pilot and co-pilot turned and looked first at me and then at each other. They then looked back out to the front of the aircraft. Neither one said another word until they requested clearance to land in La Ceiba

The others had not made it back to the plane yet, so the doctor and I spread out our gear under the wing and tried to get comfortable as we waited for the night to fall. The rain had missed the La Ceiba area, and the sky became a mass of brilliant stars. I lay there praising the Creator who had put each one of the stars into place, and who had reached down and poked His finger into the clouds to provide a way of escape for us.

My attention was drawn to a figure walking toward us from the air terminal. As the man became more visible through the darkness, I could see he had a smile on his face. In each hand he held two paper plates. He handed one plate to the doctor and the other to me. On each one was a hamburger and fried potatoes. The doctor thanked him in Spanish. The man waved and walked back through the darkness to the terminal. The doctor told me that the man ran the terminal's snack shop and he had seen us out on the field. He figured we would like something to eat. He knew we were Americans, and he just wanted to thank us for our help in the only way he knew how.

We ate everything on the plate and thanked God for again taking care of us, just as He said He would: "Do not be anxious, saying, 'What shall we eat?' or 'What shall we drink?' or' With what shall we clothe ourselves?'...for your Heavenly Father knows that you need all these things" (Matthew 6:31-32).

I was surprised I hadn't heard the approach of someone else who now stood in our midst. He was a boy of about thirteen or fourteen. His clothing was tattered and dirty, and the dirt on his face was visible even in the dim light. He said nothing, but only stood there looking at us. I reached into my pack and pulled out several packets of buffalo jerky and handed them to him. He eagerly took them. He then sat down on the ground and began eating the contents. I reached back into the pack again and pulled out a couple of cans of sardines. I didn't know if he

knew how to open the cans, so I slid over to where
he sat and pointed to the can's key and then I
opened the can and handed it to him. As he finished
the sardines, he placed the other can into his pants
pocket. I had no more, but I gave him several more
packets of jerky.

The doctor spoke to him in the boy's native
tongue, and learned that the boy had lost his family
when the flooding waters swept away his house.
Only he had survived. He had nowhere to go and no
one to turn to for help.

The boy wadded up his coat and placed it on the
ground. He then lay his head down and curled into
the fetal position. In a short time his breathing
changed to the slow steady rhythm of deep slumber.

It was now about 10:00 P.M., and we were fa-
tigued from the day's activities. We stretched out as
well and drifted off to sleep with the soft tropical
breeze blowing over us.

I awoke as the first fingers of light stretched out
over the mountains. I looked at my watch. It was a
little after 5:00 A.M. The airfield tarmac wasn't very
soft and I was stiff all over. I rolled over. The doctor
was still asleep. I looked to where the boy had been
laying — only the wind occupied the space where he
had slept. I looked around the area, but he was no
where to be found. The words of Hebrews 13:2 came
to mind: "Do not neglect to show hospitality to
strangers, for by this some have entertained angels
without knowing it." Had we entertained an angel?
Did God send one to find out how we would treat
him?

A short time after 6:00 A.M. several others of our
group came, and more arrived a short time later.

Now we were missing only four, but we still had plenty of time before we had to leave. We were all anxious to share our experiences with one another.

At 7:50 the four still hadn't arrived. With great reluctance we climbed aboard and began preparing to take off. The door was closed and the engines were started. We sat for a while as the engines warmed up. Then we began to slowly taxi toward the main runway. From the front of the plane someone yelled to stop the plane — "I see them coming!" We all jammed our faces to the window and watched four figures running toward us, waving their arms as they ran. The pilot stopped the plane and someone else opened the back door. The four climbed aboard and lay in a heap on the floor. We were all laughing and shouting as we finally made our way back to our seats.

The co-pilot leaned into the aisle and said, "Get belted in — the tower's getting angry again!" Then he added, "Our next stop, with any luck, will be the state of Texas."

The plane roared down the runway and suddenly we were airborne. As we circled the city to get going in the right direction, the plane once more fell silent as we gazed down on the still burning funeral fires.

While flying northward, we began telling of the things that had happened to each of us — story after story of how God had reached down His mighty hand and intervened for someone's welfare, and how He had touched and changed each of our lives.

As we neared El Paso, the sun had already slipped below the westerly horizon. Only a few rays of light reached up to our plane. As we neared the city's airport the pilot began talking with the tower operator and getting clearance for a landing. We were still quite a ways out, so the tower asked where we had been. The pilot briefly told him the story. The tower operator asked how many of us were on board and our pilot answered him. There was a short period of silence; then the tower operator came back on and said they were having an old-fashioned Texas barbecue at the terminal, complete with steaks, chili and French bread, and they wanted us to be their guests!

We relished the homestyle cooking and the friendly people who were so anxious to hear our stories. We got a good night's sleep, and in the morning we took off on the final leg of our flight.

We landed home in San Jose in the dark. Friends and family were waiting for us as we got out of the plane. Maggie and Michele were there and we hugged and hugged. In the car on the ride home I told Maggie about all that had happened.

We got home and I unpacked my clothing. After a long shower, I crawled into bed. Maggie and I prayed and talked for a while.

As I lay there my thoughts returned to Honduras — the medical clinic, the people, the life and the death that had been a part of my life for a week. The week seemed like an eternity, yet it also seemed like only a moment.

Then I thought about another moment, and the tears rolled down my cheeks — that moment a week earlier when God tapped me on my shoulder and whispered in my ear, "Whom shall I send, and who will go for Us?" And he placed in my heart the answer: "Here am I! Send me!"

Maybe the price of being a cop <u>was</u> too high...

Thinking of Life

★

I TOLD MAGGIE I would be gone about an hour, then left to complete some errands. When I returned, she and the girls came out to meet me as I got out of the car. Maggie asked if I had been listening to the news, and I told her no. She said a news bulletin on TV reported that two San Jose police officers had been shot — one was killed instantly and the other was listed in critical condition. She said no details were given of the shooting, and the two officers weren't named.

I felt the hot flash of adrenaline shoot through my body as I hurried inside and grabbed the telephone. I had trouble remembering what the phone number was for the main police desk, then became frustrated when I received a busy signal. I continued dialing until I finally reached an officer manning the phones. After I identified myself, I asked what had happened.

He told me the two men's names and gave some details of the shooting. I felt the strength leave my body as the realization sank in: A fellow officer and friend had been killed, and another was critically wounded.

"What type of blood do you have?" the desk officer asked. "They need blood for transfusions during the operation."

I didn't have the right type that was needed. I hung up the phone, feeling a sense of helplessness.

The news media broadcast the appeal for blood for the injured officer, and soon lines of cars were parked outside the hospital as concerned citizens and officers from other agencies came to donate their blood.

I stayed by the radio and television the rest of the afternoon, listening for information. On the televised six o'clock news, as a broadcaster described the shooting scene and the events that led up to it, I watched footage taken at the scene earlier in the day. My heart raced as the camera focused on a yellow blanket covering the slain officer's body. Beneath the blanket was the unmistakable white stripe running the length of our uniform's pants. From one side of the blanket, an arm protruded, lying motionless on the ground. This wasn't Hollywood; this was real life — and real death.

The picture changed to a live broadcast outside the hospital where the other officer had been taken. The news announcer said word had just been received that the other officer had died while in surgery.

I felt as if I were in a dream, and I was anxious to wake up so I could see that all this was unreal. But in my heart I knew it was no dream. Two police officers were dead. They weren't the first officers to die in the line of duty in San Jose, and I knew in my heart they wouldn't be the last. But this was the first time the department had lost two officers at once, and the violent way in which it happened brought a feeling of shock to the entire city.

I looked across at Maggie and the girls, and wondered if being a police officer was worth the risk that was present each time I walked out the front door of our home on my way to work. Was it fair to them for me to take those risks that go with pinning a star over my heart and carrying a gun at my side? Wasn't my nineteen years as a police officer long enough to have taken such risks? Maybe the people who had said to me over the years that they wouldn't do my job for a million dollars were right. Maybe the price of being a cop *was* too high.

But if so, who would be cops? Who would be there to answer the calls for help when the assailant attacks or the lost child needs to be found? Who would make it safe to drive the highways or walk the streets? Who would be willing to stand between the criminal and the law-abiding citizen? If not me, who?

I knew I couldn't expect anyone else to be a cop if I were unwilling — especially since I knew that being a policeman was what God wanted me to be.

And I knew I could rest in the wisdom of His will.

Six days later, the funeral for the two officers was held. Only a few months earlier I had been in the honor guard for the last San Jose officer to die in the line of duty — in a motorcycle accident — and I was asked to be in this one too. I could still remember the pain of loss I felt during that first funeral. And now, I again stood at attention in my dress uniform, in front of the same large church. But this time there were *two* flag-draped coffins being slowly carried past me, two coffins that held the bodies of fellow officers gunned down in the streets that they had sworn to defend. Two officers who had gotten up that morning thinking it would be just another day for them, doing the same job they had done for years. Another day assisting people when they called for help. Another day of taking reports and perhaps writing tickets. Another day to maybe laugh along

with the other officers during the morning briefing
session. Neither of them thought their day would
end in a hail of gunfire that would leave them dead.

As we followed the coffins into the auditorium, I
thought about my early morning routine on work-
days: Bible study and prayer time; packing my
lunch, and slipping into the lunchbox the note that
my daughter writes me everyday; kissing Maggie
goodby as I walked out the door; and flashing my
cars lights three times as an "I love you" sign, as I
wave and drive away. I rarely if ever think that I
might not be coming home that evening...

It took nearly thirty minutes for the 4,500 police
officers from more than two hundred agencies
throughout California to file into the church. Some
stood in the halls, while others stood outside and listened to the service on loud-speakers.

The police chaplain gave a fitting message for the
two officers. Then an officer got up and gave a eulogy
to his fallen friend. When he sat down, an officer's
wife stepped in front and began singing:

> *When peace like a river attendeth my way,*
>
> *when sorrows like sea billows roll;*
>
> *whatever my lot, Thou hast taught me to say,*
>
> *"It is well, it is well with my soul."*

As I stood soaking in the words to one of my favorite hymns, I knew that it *was* truly well with my
soul. The pain of the loss would stay for a long time,
the memories would continue, and questions about
the tragedy would go unanswered — but God would
still be in control, always and forever.

The service ended and the thousands of officers

filed past the coffins. Many stopped and gave a farewell salute to their fallen comrades, then waited outside the church as the coffins were brought out for the last time. As part of the honor guard I helped fold the flags to be given to our police chief, who then presented them to the officers' families.

As the sound of the twenty-one gun salute faded away, taps were played. The notes echoed off of the surrounding hills as if a distance bugler were returning the tribute to the dead. Again I remembered giving this goodby to a fellow officer only months before: the Scriptures had been read, the songs had been sung, the salutes had been given, the guns had been sounded, the folded flag had been presented. And taps had been played.

Now again, the last tears fell to the ground and clung to the grass like morning dew. I stood in silence and thought about death. I found that that the thought drew me closer to Jesus, the Giver and Keeper of life.

And the words echoed within: "It is well with my soul."

★

David R. Johnson
Post Office Box 18661
San Jose, California 95158

for information regarding Family Life Conferences:

Family Ministry
Post Office Box 23840
Little Rock, Arkansas 72221-3840
telephone: (501) 223-8663